The Stand Up Paddle Book

The complete Stand Up Paddle
Surf Guide from Window
Shopping to catching
Your First Waves

FIRST EDITION

Written and Illustrated by
Nate Burgoyne

LRP

Lava Rock Publishing
Haleiwa - Oahu - Hawaii

Published by:
Lava Rock Publishing
P.O. Box 706 Haleiwa, HI 96712
www.lavarockpublishing.com

The Stand Up Paddle Book

ISBN-13: 978-0-61542-991-5
ISBN-10: 0-61542-991-2

First Edition

These books may be purchased in bulk for retail
sales, educational purposes, sales promotions,
making paper airplanes, starting campfires and
other reasonable causes. Please direct all
inquiries to the publisher. Thank you.

For Heidi and my girls.

Table of Contents

Foreword   I

Introduction   1

Congratulations!   2
The Early Days of Surfing   7
Your First Paddle-Out   9

Section I. Safety First   11

Safety & Etiquette   12
Making New Friends in the Lineup   13
New Equipment Changes the Pace   14
$142 a Pop for Those Babies!   16
The Limits of Your New Board & Paddle   17
Where Should I Practice?   19
Don't Pee Into the Wind   21
Know & Respect Your Ability   23
Understanding the Area Inside & Out   24
Buy a New Board One Quarter at a Time   26
Green, Yellow, & Red Zones   27
Rocks & Shallow Reef   30
Surfing with Swimmers   31
Understanding Currents   32
Navigating Currents in the Surf Zone   34
Help a Brother or Sister Out   35
The Right Way to Enter the Water   37
A Wide Paddle Out   38
Approaching the Lineup   39
Nothing to Prove, Homies!   41
Small Talk   41
Even the Cat Falls Off the Fence   43
Who Has Right of Way?   44
Locking Up the Grabber   45
The California Take-Off   46
Respecting the Locals   46
The Wrap Up   47

Section II. Fitness Intro   49

Fitness to the Core   50
Fine Tuning Your Balance   51

Section III. Wave Watch   53

The Wave   54
Beach Breaks   55
Point Breaks   56
Reef Versus Sand   57
The Perfect Wave   57

Section IV. Gearing up for Surf   59

Understanding How Your Board Works   60
Virtual Training Wheels   61
Board Size & Manageability for Women   64
Nose Rocker   66
Board Thickness   67
The One Stick Quiver   69
Bottom Contour   70
Hard & Soft Rails   71
The Deck   73
Tail Rocker   75
A Variety of Tail Shapes   76
Board Construction   78
Your Are Board Savvy. Now What?   83

Section V. Fins and More Fins   85

Fins Can Make All the Difference   86
The Single Fin Setup   87
Versatile 2+1 Fin Setup   90
Roaring Thruster Setups   92
Twin Fins, Quads & More   94
Testing the Stock Fins   95
Screwing in the Fins   96
Staring Into the Fin Crystal Ball   97

Section VI. The Bells and Whistles   99

Accessories   100
Why a Deck Pad?   101
The Right Leash for SUP Surfing   104
Leash Anatomy   106
Leash or No Leash   108

Section VII. Paddle Picking Time   111

The Perfect Paddle   112
Driving Flat Blades   114
Not the Broom!   *116*
Smooth Dihedral Blades   117
The Coveted Carbon Fiber Paddle   118
Fiberglass Paddles   120
Wood Paddles Full of Soul   121
Indestructible Aluminum   122
Indexed Paddle Shafts   123
Paddle Handle Options   124
Face-Whacked! Wax That Handle   *126*
Paddle Height   127

Section VIII. Getting Out & Getting Up   131

Carrying Your Board   132
Before You Put Your Board in the Water   139
Two Ways to Get on Your Board   140
Super SUPaddle Guy   142
Two Ways to Easily Stand Up   144
The Stability Checklist   *147*
White-Knuckle, Death-Grip Toe Pain   147
A Stylish Dismount   148
Just in Case You Happen to Fall Off   149

Section IX: Stance & Posture   153

The Essentials   154
Correct Posture Right from the Start   154
The Most Stable Stance   155

The Staggered Stance   157
The Surf Stance Dance   158

Section X: Paddle & Board Control   161

Paddling & Turning Like a Champ   162
Gripping the Paddle   164
The Forward Stroke   165
Can I Paddle Straight?   169
The Left or Right Side?   172
Short Strokes or Long Strokes?   173
One-Stroke One-Eighties   174
Smooth Standing Turns   175
Busting Quick Kick Turns   176
Wave Take-Offs in Flat Water   178
Keeping Watch Over Your Shoulder   180

Section XI: Ready for Surf   181

Have Control, Give Respect & Get Waves   182
Don't Be a Cocked Pistol   183
Prone-Paddle Surfing Before SUP Surfing?   184
Kissed by a Wave   185
Reading the Waves   188
Positioning & Stability   189
The Backward Suck & Forward Push   191
The Need for Speed   193
Making the Drop Safely & Totally Committed   195
Take the Blinders Off   *197*
Attacking the Bottom Turn   198
Which Way is Left? Which Way is Right?   *200*
Flip the Blade or Leave it Straight?   *202*
What to Do With Your Paddle While Surfing   202
Let them Hang: Noserides   204
Cross Stepping   206
Fat Stand Up Paddle Floaters   207
A New Beginning   209

Section XII: Taking on the Elements   211

Surfing in Less than Perfect Conditions   212

Managing the Wind   213
Blessed Off-Shore Wind   215
Using Side-Shore Wind to Your Advantage   217
Making the Most of On-Shore Wind   219
The Dynamics of Variable Wind   220
Be Thankful for the Wind   221

Section XIII: Wipeout Survival Guide   223

Wipeouts & Getting Caught Inside   224
Trouble Ahead? Safety First   226
Surviving Wipeouts with a Paddle   227
You're Caught Inside: Now What?   229
Retaining Your Board: Tail Grab   232
Another Technique: Leash Wrap   233
After the Set Waves Have Passed   234
Losing Your Board in the Surf   236
Swimming with Your Paddle   237

Section: XIV: The Conclusion   241

Section XV: The Fitness Appendix   245

Really Going for it With Moderation   246
Cross Training at Home   247
Lower Body Strength Training   248
Upper Body Resistance Training   251

Section XVI: Glossary of Key Terms   251

About the Author   265
Special Thanks   266
Super Awesome Bonus   267
Contact Us   267
The Next Edition   267

Join *The Stand Up Paddle Book Crew*   See Back

FOREWORD

"In a cyber age where any fool with a keyboard can become an instant expert on stand up paddling, Nate Burgoyne is a breath of fresh air.

On a huge day at Sunset Beach, I watched him charge the giants. Nate Burgoyne has the guts and game to back up his words. Aloha."

Dave Chun
Shaper & Founder
Kialoa Paddles
www.kialoa.com

"Stand up paddling has changed many people's lives. For some, it's the benefits of better health. For some, it's a way to become connected with nature. For some, the surfing aspect is unbeatable.

One thing is for sure; for all, it is fun!

This clear and easy to read book is a great resource that takes you step-by-step so you can get out on the water and enjoy stand up paddling. Nate does a beautiful job of keeping things simple to understand and easy to read.

In no time, you too will be out there enjoying what others have found to be the best all around core workout that is so fun you forget you are working out! Aloha."

Blane Chambers
Shaper and Founder
Paddle Surf Hawaii
www.paddlesurfhawaii.com

"Stand up paddling will change your body and your life. For many of us passionate paddlers out here in Hawaii, it's what we are fortunate enough to do for a living.

As a personal trainer I am always astounded by the positive body and mind transformations I've seen both personally and with my clients since I've implemented stand up paddling into my workout programs.

If you are interested in making this transformation for yourself, then this book is a great place to start.

Nate has laid out the basics in an easy to understand, comprehensive, and humorous book that you will find helpful in your endeavors to hone in on your paddling skills, be safe, and not be a 'kook'.

Also included are basic conditioning exercises and helpful advice to give you the muscle strength and endurance needed to enjoy longer sessions on the water!

You will need the stamina because stand up paddling is so much fun you will not realize that hours have gone by and you're getting the workout of your life!"

Nikki Gregg, CPT
SUP Personal Trainer
NRG Lifestyles Fitness
www.nikkigregg.com

INTRODUCTION

CONGRATULATIONS!

You have in front of you a complete guide to stand up paddle surfing etiquette, equipment, and surfing technique! Whether you're just starting out or are an experienced stand up paddle surfer, get ready for an awesome journey the sport of stand up paddle surfing.

This book is packed with as many tips, tricks, guidelines, and good times as I could possibly squeeze between the first and last pages. It was a thrill putting it together and when I think about it, my heart still pounds with excitement!

Why? I know that the techniques, knowledge, and insights within these pages will take stand up paddlers of varying abilities to a new level of performance. By reading this book, your learning curve will be accelerated as you review the easy-to-follow explanations and diagrams, and mentally prepare yourself for the water.

Once again, veteran surfers are back in the water, giddy as school children, catching their first waves and having more fun than a barrel of monkeys in a banana pie factory. From lazy ankle-high waves to overhead bombs, stand up paddling is all about pure, unrestricted fun.

Why has this sport captivated the worldwide surfing and fitness communities?

Maybe it's the ability to surf waves away from the crowds. It could possibly be the never-ending sensation of walking on water. Maybe it's the unbelievable core workout. Perhaps it's the thrill of the hunt for new waves never ridden before, or maybe it's the calm serenity of staring out into an endless horizon.

For you, it could be the challenge of connecting the mind and the body in perfect harmony, resulting in some of the most gracefully radical lines ever drawn on the face of a wave.

Whatever the underlying reason, it is easy to become hooked on this amazing sport. Now, what do you have to look forward to in the coming pages?

In the early sections this book, you'll find a brief history of the sport. When you know where you come from it gives more meaning to where you are going.

Then, we'll discuss etiquette and safety. With big boards and paddles being introduced to surfing lineups around the world, it is essential to address the issues of stand up paddle surfing etiquette to keep everyone safe and to preserve the good name of the sport.

Later, you will learn everything from what you can do to condition yourself for stand up paddle surfing to what equipment is best suited for your local surf. You'll also get the scoop on SUP surfboard design and construction, paddles, leashes, deck pads, and accessories so you can gear up with exactly what you need.

In this book, you'll also find paddling and surfing techniques that will take you to a level you may currently think is impossible on a stand up paddle surfboard.

The Stand Up Paddle Book is loaded with insider tips to help you get the most out of your time on the water.

Should you read this book cover to cover or just pick out sections? It's totally up to you.

Stand up paddle surfing is not a linear process at all and neither is this book. I wrote the book to be read either way. Your foot position affects your arms, and your arms affect your balance, and your balance determines your power, and your power influences your ability to catch waves and make the most of them, and all of that is being continually altered by the ever-changing wind and sea.

There are so many things going on simultaneously while paddling and catching waves that, to really grasp everything, you'll want to read *all* the chapters.

On one final note before we begin, so long as there are waves to be ridden, advances in equipment and discoveries in technique will be constantly evolving and progressing.

I sincerely hope you enjoy your journey through the *First Edition* of *The Stand Up Paddle Book* which is neither the beginning, nor the end, but stoke in progress. *Here we go. Enjoy the book!*

Wait! Before you go any further

Choose your FREE SUP STICKER with your FREE MEMBERSHIP to *The Stand Up Paddle Book Crew!*

www.standuppaddlebook.com/crew

Now you can read *The Stand Up Paddle Book* with other stand up paddlers around the world online. I'm serious! No joke! Really!!!

This is a book without covers!

Every chapter of this book has its own discussion where you can comment, ask questions, and share your own personal insights and thoughts with other readers as you read this book. Pretty sweet!

Bonus! As the lucky purchaser of this book, when you join *The Stand Up Paddle Book Club* you will also choose your FREE STAND UP PADDLE STICKER while supplies last!

And since you're getting a free sticker... you can tell all your friends that you're sponsored!

Simply go to:
www.standuppaddlebook.com/crew
and join the crew.

THE EARLY DAYS OF SURFING

There are many theories about exactly when and where stand up paddling first began. While the stories may vary, there is a consensus that some of the beginnings date back to the Waikiki beach boys of the 1960s from which the sport derived the nickname of "beach-boy style surfing."

During the 1960s the world went crazy for surfing! Surf films, surf music and the mass production of surfboards began a never-ending tidal wave of excitement for the sport that is sure to continue forever.

What used to be a small group of watermen soon became thousands of surfers around the world searching for rideable waves.

During this time period, the original Hawaiian beach boys spent their time busily giving surf lessons in Waikiki on the south shore of Oahu to tourists from across the globe.

Naturally, when a tourist would journey to Hawaii to learn how to surf, a photo of the event was a must-have memento to show off to the friends back home.

What better way to capture the good times than an up-close action photograph taken by someone along side them in the water?

Thus, some of the early beach boys would be seen with cameras in hand, gliding across the water on stand up paddle surfboards to shoot the perfect souvenir for those having their first surf lessons. Since this was long before waterproof water housings were available, stand up paddling was a useful way to keep the camera high and dry.

Now, the lazy days of stand up paddle surfboards for tourist photo ops in the rolling waves of Waikiki has evolved into a thrilling sport practiced by some of the world's greatest athletes as it continues to spread like crazy throughout the oceans, rivers, and lakes of the Americas, Asia, Europe, Australia, Africa, and the islands of the Pacific. This worldwide sport knows no boundaries. We can only imagine where the sport will take us next.

A MAGICAL PADDLE-OUT

Nobody can forget the first time they paddled out on a stand up paddle board. Whether it's an easy paddle out on a smooth lake or a challenging crash course in breath-holding and swimming, without fail, it's always magical.

For me, it was another a calm and sunny morning on the North Shore of Oahu and I was doing my best to awkwardly balance a stand up paddle board on my head.

A short walk through the trees and over golden sand and I found myself at the water's edge. I delicately slid the board into the water. Paddle in hand, I eased myself on top of the board, kneeling. With a deep breath and a smile I said to myself, "Well, here it goes." I brought my feet under me, straightened my back, and *I was standing*.

There I was, hovering above the water in the still of the harbor for the first time - pure satisfaction. It was about 10:30 in the morning and the sun shone straight through the crystal clear water revealing the watery world just below my feet.

After a gentle stroke on one side of the board, I brought the paddle around to the other side and ever so delicately sliced the paddle into the water as if the surface tension of the ocean was holding the world together.

The thrill of the moment that I had felt years ago after catching my first waves as a prone-paddle surfer, all at once came flooding back to me and ran from my toes to my fingertips, and I hadn't even caught a wave yet!

One even stroke after another, the board and paddle whisked me away from the shore like a magic carpet ride sailing above the mosaic of the ocean floor below me. I was instantly hooked.

After that, I was totally converted to stand up paddling. My regular surfboards all went into retirement as I founded the digital magazine *Stand Up Paddle Surfing Magazine (www.supsurfmag.com)*, the world's first stand up paddle publication, and spent the coming years trying to figure out how to do this awesome sport and share the stoke of it with others around the globe.

It was then when I started writing *The Stand Up Paddle Book* and later co-founded *Rainbow Watersports Adventures* stand up paddle school *(www.rainbowwatersports.com)* at home in Hawaii on the North Shore of Oahu.

Yep, it pretty much took over my life and I've loved every minute of it. My story is not unique. Imagine where this sport will take you, too!

Section I.
SAFETY FIRST

SAFETY & ETIQUETTE

A safe and respectful lineup is a happy lineup, and proper etiquette and respect means good times for everyone in the water. Safety should be foremost on every stand up paddler's mind when entering the ocean.

Throughout this book, you will find tons of essential safety tips. Remember them and, most importantly, use them! Anyone who has ever been hit by a surfboard of any kind, or who has simply had a close call, will agree that a lesson in safety is the first place to start.

If you are the first stand up paddle surfer at your home break, the dynamics of adding a stand up paddle surfer to the lineup will be new to everyone in the water. With a stand up board, you may sometimes feel like you're on stage. Well, the reality is you probably are.

Others may be watching you out of curiosity to see if it's something they'll want to try out one day, while others may gaze in your direction simply because there's nothing else to look. Don't worry about it, just relax, be friendly, have fun, and obey the rules.

When you adhere to the guidelines of safety and etiquette we'll be discussing, you'll be catching waves and bringing good vibes and smiles to the lineup.

MAKING NEW FRIENDS IN THE LINEUP

The first rule for any stand up paddle surfers is to be friendly on the beach and in the water. With a smile on your face and a pleasant disposition, curious surfers and beachgoers will often approach you to ask questions about your board and how you like the sport. Take a minute or two to chat with them. You'll be able to share your excitement and bring good vibes to your local surf spot.

When you're out in the water, compliment other surfers on their waves and be stoked for them. Alert them of the incoming set waves. Your elevated field of vision will allow you to see them before anyone else. So, when you see a bomb set approaching, give a holler.

Some have recommended offering to switch equipment with other surfers in the lineup to let traditional surfers have a try at stand up paddling for themselves. Use discretion and good judgment if you choose to loan your board out. Even an experienced surfer is going to be somewhat out of control on his or her first waves.

If someone takes you up on your offer to trade equipment and wants to give it a try, take that person to a wave away from the crowd or off into the flat water will ensure a safe and fun time for everyone.

NEW EQUIPMENT CHANGES THE PACE

If you are coming from a traditional prone paddle surfing background, the pace changes when you take up stand up paddling. For some, the pace seems to go much more quickly on a stand up paddle board while, for others, things seem to move more slowly. Anyone who has ever switched from a traditional longboard surfboard to a short prone-paddle surfboard or vice-versa knows what I'm talking about. Personally, I learned this the hard way back several years ago.

Years before I got hooked on stand up paddling, I was an avid prone-paddle longboarder. One afternoon, a shortboarder friend of mine wanted to swap boards with me for a while so he could give my longboard a try. Some time on a shortboard sounded like fun, so we swapped boards.

Shortly thereafter, I found myself paddling for the horizon as a rogue set wave approached. Although I was well aware of proper surfing etiquette, I was unfamiliar with the speed at which I could paddle that shortboard.  As the set approached, I looked toward the break and noticed a longboard surfer on the wave. It was a situation I had been in countless times before, but on a different board.

All of a sudden the surfer's big red board came straight at me as I dove underwater and covered my head to make an escape, but to no avail. I got tagged in the head by his big fin and it took a trip to the hospital and 14 staples in my scalp to close it all up. I sure was lucky to have made it through that one.

$142 A POP FOR THOSE BABIES!

On a side note, for those who are wondering: 14 staples in the scalp costs about $2,000 without insurance, without a ride in the ambulance, and if you can talk the doctor into giving you a staple remover so you can get them out yourself. That's almost 143 bucks a staple! Maybe they're platinum. I still have those staples somewhere. I just can't bring myself to toss 'em in the trash. I think I'll string them into a necklace or something.

Some said that the surfer did a trick when he shouldn't have, but in my mind, I wonder if the error was on my end, not knowing the speed at which I could paddle the shorter board to get me from point A to point B. Maybe it was I who put myself in the wrong place at the wrong time because I was unfamiliar with the equipment I was riding. The same holds true for new stand up paddlers.

The point is, even if you have a surfing background, as you enter the water with other surfers and are learning to ride waves, the timing of the ocean and the rhythm of the lineup are going to be much different than you have been used to.

Even accomplished surfers will have a period of adjustment as they learn how their stand up paddle equipment turns, accelerates, and responds, both in flat water, in the lineup, and on the waves.

Make sure you take the time to get familiar with your equipment before surfing with others. Practice paddle sprints in flat water and distance paddles in open ocean swells until you become well acquainted with your personal ability and the limitations of your equipment.

Have the discipline to talk with other stand up paddlers to find out how they would approach certain situations. Then, when the time comes that you have to make a critical decision in the water, you'll know how to make the right one.

Whether it means taking another day, week, month, or year to refine your skills in flat water before entering a surf zone, always do what it takes to keep everyone safe. Remember that there will always be another wave and there will always be another swell.

Now, let's get down to the nitty gritty. . .

THE LIMITS OF YOUR NEW BOARD & PADDLE

Your stand up paddle surfboard is probably the meatiest board in your quiver. It carries with it more momentum and volume than any other board you may have ever ridden.

17

Avoid playing bumper boards with other surfers by intuitively knowing where the nose and tail of your board end, how long your leash is, and how far your paddle can reach. When you instinctively know where your equipment begins and ends, you'll be able to keep a safe distance from others.

Casual paddling and surfing small waves will help you get to know your board. However, if you want to cut to the chase and quickly master your gear, here's what you can do. It might sound silly, but paddle out in some flat water and walk straight off the nose. Climb back on your board and walk backwards straight off the tail.

Next, slide your feet to the side edges of the board and wobble the board side to side until you flip it over, familiarizing yourself with your board's stability. In doing this exercise, you'll probably discover that your stand up paddle board is actually quite stable and that it takes quite an effort to actually flip upside down. What this means is a great part of the instability you may presently feel comes from you, not the equipment.

Next, Get in the water and push your board to the end of your leash. Take note of the distance between you and the furthest part of your board then add at least 20 yards to it. In the surf, a wave will stretch your leash and wash you and your board a lot further than you probably think.

Repeat all of these until you instinctively know where your board starts and ends to discover how far you need to steer clear of others in the water to avoid any type of collision if you happen to fall off.

Looking ahead to performance surfing, by walking off the nose, you'll know how many steps it'll take to get up there for a noseride. By walking off the tail, you'll learn how far you can step back before sliding off the back. And I'm telling you, one of the scariest sights you'll ever see is when slipping off the back of the board, you watch the tail of your board rising up to meet you "where the sun don't shine." Seriously, world goes into slow motion as your mind says, "Nnnnoo-o-o-o-o!"

When you take the time to familiarize yourself with your equipment, you're also establishing a strong foundation for further development of your flat water and wave riding skills.

WHERE SHOULD I PRACTICE?

Whether you are refining your basic skills or learning a new trick, practice away from others. We all fall off when we're practicing; it's how we improve. Steer clear of other surfers during these practice sessions so that neither you nor your equipment lands on anyone.

Your first experience on a stand up paddle surfboard should be in flat water. Lakes, rivers, and harbors are great places for this. If you don't have such a place nearby, or if your local surf break is the only option, consider waking up extra early to be the first person out in the water before the crowd arrives.

I've found that if I'm waiting in the parking lot in the morning when it's still dark, and if I get in the water when it's just light enough to see, I can usually surf alone, or with just one or two fellow surfers long before the "before-work" crowd arrives.

If you start your session just as the sun comes up, by the time the lineup is overcrowded, you probably will have gotten your fill of waves for the day and will be ready to head home.

The real challenge you'll have if you're out on your own and the surf is firing, will be trying to decide how good to make the waves look out there. When you see people lined up on the beach watching to see how the waves are, you'll probably have a little angel on one shoulder saying, "Go for it! It's a beautiful wave. Tear it up." And on the other shoulder you'll have a little devil saying, "Hold back a little. Don't make it look too good. If you do, they're all going to paddle out." Well, I must admit, the little angel wins out every time for me.

Once the crowd paddles out, you can also have a blast on the "junk" waves that other surfers pass up. You may even discover a new "secret spot" that seems like it was built especially for stand up paddle surfing.

I'm telling you, you can have so much fun just paddling around in circles or cruising up and down the coast. With stand up paddle surfing, you don't have to surf or paddle where everyone else flocks to. It is easy to go catch waves at places that are too far for prone-paddle surfers to paddle out to, or in places that have been put aside for years by the mainstream crowd.

DON'T PEE INTO THE WIND

For lack of a better way to put it, here's one tip I think you'll find useful as you're getting familiar with your new equipment in small surf, and that is, "Don't pee into the wind." Why? Because what goes into the wind comes right back at you. It's a lesson that you most guys need to learn only once.

What does peeing into the wind have to do with stand up paddle surfing?

It means that when you are caught in the impact zone off your board with rows of whitewater coming at you, regardless of the wave height, do your best to keep your board and paddle between you and the beach, and not between you and the incoming waves.

With your board between you and the waves, even the energy from little ankle snapping waves can cause your board or paddle to give you a good knock in the head if you're not paying attention.

And, how do you think I learned that?

You got it. I took a stiff board knock on the noggin.

KNOW & RESPECT YOUR ABILITY

The day will soon arrive when you wake up in the morning, bright eyed and full of energy, and the little voice in your head will say, "You're ready. Today's the day. It's time to venture out into the waves." When that day arrives, be mindful of your ability, and surf within it.

While you're working on getting your bearings straight, stay out of the main lineup and surf where you understand how the water and wind currents flow and where you know that you will be able to swim back to the beach should your board or leash break in the water.

If big waves or outer reefs are what you're chasing, take a friend, or ideally two. Then, in the event of an emergency one can tend to the other while the third goes for help.

Be responsible enough to recognize that although you may have been confident in the pack on a prone paddle surfboard yesterday, today you're on a new piece of equipment and are figuring out how it works.

Stand up paddle surfing may be a humbling experience at first, but smile and have fun with it. After all, the best surfer isn't the one catching the most waves; it's the one having the most fun.

UNDERSTANDING THE AREA INSIDE & OUT

Have you ever noticed how there are some surfers that are always in the right spot at the right time and rarely get caught in the impact zone? For some reason they are able to stay out of danger and help others who may be in trouble. How do they learn all this? They learn from talking to others, carefully observing the conditions, and spending time both on, and under, the water.

You'll see these watermen and waterwomen watching the waves from the shore for hours at a time studying the angles and movement of the water. They understand how the water moves and how it will change the wave when it hits a certain section of the reef or sand bar.

When the waves are down, these surfers are out in the ocean diving beneath the water to memorize how the reef and rocks are laid out so as to understand from the inside out the anatomy of each wave from the ocean floor to its foamy crest. There's something to be learned from this.

Before you slide your board into the water, take the time to talk with the local surfers or lifeguards about how the waves in the area form and break.

You'll find that there are certain surf spots where the waves jack up quickly and there are others where the waves slowly form as they move in. Take the time to get educated about the waves you are looking at. It will help you be safe and catch waves.

On that note, while you are watching from the beach, survey the scene for any potentially dangerous obstacles and situations. And then when you get in the water, hang back, watch the waves, and identify the shallow spots and hazards.

BUY A NEW BOARD ONE QUARTER AT A TIME

When you take the time to survey the ocean floor in the off-season, you'll be stoked on all free stuff you'll find down there. Rarely do I go for an off-season dive at our local breaks and not come up with free goggles, surfboard fins, a swim fin, or some spare change. Although I haven't been fortunate enough to find a diamond ring, I do know people who have found such treasures. Save it all up and you may just end up funding your new board one quarter at a time, or at least enough for a burrito when you're done with your dive!

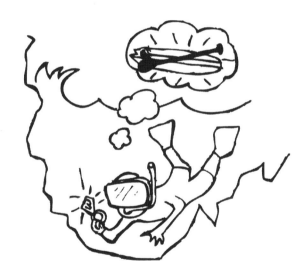

GREEN, YELLOW & RED ZONES

One way of keeping yourself oriented in the water is to categorize areas of the surf zone by color: green, yellow, and red. Green zones are those that can always be considered safe. Yellow zones have changing variables and may quickly switch from safe to dangerous. Red zones are danger zones. Before you paddle out, identify and map out in your mind which areas of the surf zone that fit into each of these categories.

Remember that when you get in the water and are subject to the ebb and flow of moving water and other surfers, you may have to revise your mental safety map of the area.

Green areas are safety zones where the current is minimal, there are no underwater hazards, and there is little or no risk or danger of you colliding with other surfers.

Green areas are where you can rest easy knowing that the conditions in that area are not going to change when the next set of waves arrives or when the pack of surfers migrates from one area to another.

Green areas also include places where you will not be seen as a threat by others surfers who are already in the water. Green areas may include the channel next to the surf zone, the area far beyond the pack of surfers, a boat harbor, a calm section of water down the coast, or the swimming pool in your back yard.

Yellow areas are like temporary safety zones that may change with the arrival of a set of waves or with a shift of the surf lineup. When you're in a yellow zone you constantly need to be aware of your surroundings in all directions.

You may find yourself paddling in and out of yellow zones as you see an approaching set to put yourself in position to take off and ride a wave.

Yellow zones may include areas where other surfers are nearby, places near rocks or other obstacles that could become dangerous in the event of a rogue sneaker set wave, a boat channel or a field of

sea urchins, and may also include areas where you

28

could simply get caught inside after riding a wave and taking an early wipeout.

Red zones are areas to avoid at all costs for your safety and the safety of those around you. This would include sitting right in the middle of a pack of surfers, being caught between the waves and a rock or shallow reef, strong currents, boat channels, areas near the beach where swimmers or surfers could get hit by your equipment.

Stay out of the red zones. However, if things happen and you find yourself in a difficult spot, protect the safety of others first, then your own, then your equipment. Make getting out of a red zone your number one priority.

Be aware that what may have been a green zone yesterday could be a red zone today. Tides, currents, and swells are continually changing. Like the lifeguard signs always say, "If in doubt, don't go out."

ROCKS & SHALLOW REEF

It takes a trained eye to spot rocks and shallow reef from the shore. These obstacles may be just beneath the surface of the water, barely out of sight. If you spy any unusually turbulent sections of water, this is almost a sure sign of shallow reef or rocks.

Take note of any obvious hazards that the other surfers are avoiding. Mentally record where other surfers are kicking out and finishing their waves. Although it may simply be a force of habit for them to kick out of a wave early, it could also be because they know something you don't know. Perhaps there is an unseen hazard or a strong current that a newcomer would not know about.

Look for boils in the water. A boil is a round a section of water that appears as if there is a huge bubble of air just under the surface about to break through. In these boils, the water is getting channeled up toward the surface. They don't always indicate a hazard, but it's a good idea to steer clear of these  until you're able to check them out safely. If the water is clear, paddle over to it between sets and check it out.

Finally, as I just mentioned, the best thing you can do to avoid unseen obstacles is to simply ask a lifeguard for someone familiar with the area. I can't say it enough: Although stand up paddle surfing will afford you a great field of vision, it's best to check things out and ask about known hazards before paddling into the wild blue yonder, especially in high surf.

SURFING WITH SWIMMERS

Although you will have an extended field of vision while standing above the water, it is not easy to spot swimmers, snorkelers and body surfers who often seem to appear out of nowhere.

While you're on the beach, before you get in the water, mentally map out where the swimmers are and steer clear of them.

While you're in the water, scan the inside sections of the surf zone over and over for swimmers, snorkelers and others who may have unknowingly drifted into the surf.

Once you have identified what could be considered a swim zone, even though you might be able to ride your wave all the way to the sand, if there are swimmers, it's a good idea to kick out early and go catch another wave. Better safe than sorry; no wave is worth accidentally hitting someone with your board.

UNDERSTANDING CURRENTS

Moving water is one of the most powerful forces on earth. Even in a seemingly calm and pleasant harbor, there are likely to be currents either above or below the surface of the water that could send you drifting out to sea or down the coast into unfamiliar waters. Since it is in the waves and currents where the strength of the ocean is manifest, it is imperative that you understand how the currents work and how water moves before you paddle out into the ocean.

Currents are cyclical, and once you understand the cycle, you will be able to use the movement of the water to your advantage. In its simplicity, waves which start thousands of miles out in the ocean come rolling in toward the beach in a surge of energy. When the water hits a reef, sandbar or some other obstacle beneath the surface of the ocean, the water is pushed up forming a visible wave.

If you were to ride a wave at an angle all the way to where the wave ends, you would normally find yourself in what's called "the channel", where all the water flows back out to the ocean.

If you look at a channel underwater, you would likely see a deep valley in the ocean floor formed after thousands of years of water flowing through it the same way a river slowly erodes away land.

After the water arrives at the beach, it flows sideways along the coast until it can make its way back out to the ocean through a channel. This ebb and flow of the water moving in, across, and back out, is what creates the strong shore breaks and rip currents that lifeguards often post signs about.

NAVIGATING CURRENTS IN THE SURF ZONE

When navigating surf zone currents, your paddle can give you some extra power to help control your direction, but not even you and your paddle can match the energy of the ocean during a macking swell. Furthermore, if your leash or board happen to break, it'll be imperative that you work with the energy of the ocean to get back to the beach.

If you happen to get stuck in a current that is taking you either out to sea or into dangerous waters, paddle *parallel* with the shoreline until you're out of the current. This often means paddling straight into the wave impact zone. When the rip current is strong, that's where you'll want to be. The waves will push you towards the shore. You may take some big waves over the head. That's ok. They're pushing you toward the beach.

Relax and let the waves wash you in. Then, when you're near the beach, climb up on your board and paddle like mad to get to the sand. Or if you are without a board, swim hard when you get near the shore as to avoid being pulled across the beach and back out to the ocean by the cross-current along the shoreline.

Again, all the water that just pushed you in immediately starts flowing sideways and back out to the ocean after it meets the shoreline.

If you don't make it to the beach the first time around, there's a good chance that the current will sweep you sideways along the coast and back out to the ocean through the channel and you'll be back where you started. If this happens, rest on a fellow surfer's board, then try again.

HELP A BROTHER OR SISTER OUT

Now that you understand how water moves, watch for other surfers who may get stuck in the currents and might not understand how the currents flow.

A few years ago during one of the last swells of the season, there was a surfer stuck in a rip current that was taking him straight toward a rock outcropping along the beach. I paddled over to him and had him hold onto my leash as I pulled him out of the rip current.

It took three tries to get him out of that current. He was exhausted and every time I brought him right to the edge of the impact zone, he would think he was safe and let go, causing him to drift right back where he came from. Recognizing that he didn't understand how the water was moving, on the third attempt, I waited for a lull in the waves then paddled both of us right under the lip of a big one that eventually came and washed him all the way in.

In summary, be respectful of the ocean's power and ask a lifeguard or local surfer how the currents flow in your area. Then, share your newfound knowledge with others who may be struggling. Often a simple change in paddling direction can get you or someone else to safety.

The bonus is, when you understand how the currents flow, you can ride them straight out to the lineup with hardly any effort on your part. You'll be having a grand old time riding the waves in and riding the currents back out to the lineup.

THE RIGHT WAY TO ENTER THE WATER

Now, here you are. You've taken the time to scan the scene and familiarize yourself with the area. The conditions are good, you've identified the channel and it's finally time to paddle out. A good place to put your board in the water is up-current from where the water moves along the shore before flowing out to the ocean through the channel.

Basically, you'll get in the water at a place where, once you enter the water, the current that is running parallel with the beach immediately carries you sideways toward the channel that's sending the water out to sea.

While it may be a fun ride, as you drift along sideways, pay attention because if the cross current on the shoreline is strong enough there's a chance that you might overshoot the channel and get pulled over to the next surf break.

If the water entry place is somewhat rocky or unconventional, watch where the other surfers are getting in the water and the path they travel to get out to the lineup. Follow their lead.

If there are several of you waiting for the right moment to get in the water, let the other surfers get in first. That way you won't have to worry about blocking their path should you get knocked off your board by backwash from the shore break.

A WIDE PADDLE OUT

After you make it to the channel and are on your way out to sea, steer clear and wide of any other surfers that may be paddling out in front or in back of you. Give yourself plenty of room all around.

Occasionally a wave might break in the channel hurling a ball of whitewater toward you. Stand up paddle surfboards are great at punching through the whitewater up to about waist high, however beyond that you're likely to be bucked off your board.

If you take a wide path out, even if you get knocked off, you won't have to worry about your board hitting anyone next to or behind you. Also, be aware of other surfers who may choose to follow *your* path out to the lineup. Make an effort to get away from them as quickly as possible.

If a good wall of whitewater does comes down on you and you lose hold of your board, it can easily travel 30 feet or more behind you endangering anyone that may be following you out to the lineup.

You can travel great distances rather quickly on a stand up paddle surfboard. Be on the lookout for those around you and go wide to give yourself some room even if it means a few extra minutes of paddling.

APPROACHING THE LINEUP

As visible as stand up paddlers are, it's important to take your time paddling to where the surf breaks so as to not upset the balance of the lineup. Your paddle gives you so much power that you could easily pass up almost anyone else that happens to be paddling out to the surf along with you.

If you hang back and let the other surfers pass you up as you paddle out, it'll send them the message that you're not out to grab all the waves, but are simply there to enjoy the ocean and play in the surf along with everyone else.

Of course, there may be occasion when you must race to the horizon to make it over an incoming set before it breaks over you, but other than that, take it easy. Not only will you conserve energy, but those around you won't feel like you are passing them up to steal their waves. You may even want to sit or kneel on your board for some of the paddle out. Enjoy the view and let the current effortlessly carry you to where you want to be.

When you finally make it to where the waves are breaking, sit down on your board to rest and relax for a while before catching some waves. Just like they taught us in grade school, everyone has to wait their turn, and you'll have to wait yours too.

Actually, sitting on your board will usually put everyone else at ease. If you tower above the crowd, stern faced and stiff, you'll come across as lofty and intimidating. Keep it real; relax; and you'll likely become a welcome member of the regular crew.

If you don't have the patience to let waves pass to other surfers, instead of crowding the lineup, try staying more on the inside to catch the leftover waves that nobody else wanted, or go find a surf break that the other surfers aren't interested in.

NOTHING TO PROVE, HOMIES!

There's an interesting phenomenon that takes place among some beginner-intermediate stand up paddlers when they first enter a lineup or when they're joined by other stand up paddlers.

Some stand up paddlers feel an obligation to aggressively catch set waves to prove that they know what they're doing.

To me, it's down right amusing to watch another stand up paddler who has been polite and considerate in the lineup all day quickly turn into a grabber as soon as another stand up paddler starts heading out to the lineup.

If you find yourself slipping into this mindset, chill out homie. We know you're good. Experienced stand up paddlers shred when it's their turn and always respect the lineup.

SMALL TALK

As you make friends with others in the water, tensions will ease and you'll be welcome back next time. That said, small talk and making friends doesn't give you a free card to get the best waves, but it makes for a pleasant day on the water.

41

Do your best to blend in with other surfers. It may take some time. In fact, truth be told, you may have to frequent more popular breaks for a while without catching any waves before you're invited to ride waves with the local crew.

So, what in the world do you talk about with a complete stranger bobbing in the ocean? An easy topic is how the swell has changed over the last hour. Make small talk about their equipment, the day's weather, and give compliments on well ridden waves.

Most surfers are some of the most mellow, giving people you'll ever meet. Be respectful, be friendly and non-intrusive, and you'll have a great day on the water.

EVEN THE CAT FALLS OFF THE FENCE

Even when you feel like you have your basic paddling skills wired, give yourself some room in the lineup and on the wave. Hey, even a cat falls off the fence from time to time! In the lineup, when you're just hanging out waiting for the next set, unexpected bumps

in the water combined with a gust of wind and a thought about a cheeseburger can send even the best surfer for a dip into the water. Prepare for these "kook" moments by keeping a safe distance from those around you.

Likewise, give yourself some space while riding waves. Waves can change shape and direction without warning and everyone's bound to wipe out eventually. When it's your turn, you'll feel at ease knowing you're clear of other surfers and swimmers. A 12 foot board with an attenuated 12-foot leash tangled in a big ball of foam could easily reach someone up to 50 feet away.

If things get too busy in the water and you wish you could call in the surf traffic police, simply leave and go for a nice paddle down the coast to work on your flat water skills. There will always be another day and you can catch some waves next time.

43

WHO HAS RIGHT OF WAY?

In general, the surfer that is up and riding closest to the breaking part of the wave has priority on the wave. That surfer is "deepest" and in the most critical section of the wave and has the ability to accelerate out of the pocket and perform on the face of the wave. If there is a surfer coming across a wave toward you, don't drop in on that wave. If in doubt, don't go.

Also, be aware of where the prone-paddle surfers are lined up and taking off from. A prone paddle surfer may take a late drop down the wave unseen by you. They may even take off really deep with the whitewater breaking over their backs. Be aware of this.

Don't drop in on anyone!

Those on short boards sitting closer to the shore are also in the lineup; they're looking for a steeper section to take off on. When everyone is aware of everyone else, there is one big rotation among all surfers regardless of what they are riding. Without mutual respect for all wave riders, ill feelings can arise between groups of different board riders.

Dropping in on another surfer is dangerous and will probably be your ticket back to the beach. Again, there can't be enough said about the importance of observing the dynamics of the line up from the beach and from the water then slowly becoming a part of it.

Stand up paddle surfing should never be a battle of the big boards and is in no way a license to catch all the best waves that come through. Especially while you're learning the ropes, you should be shredding on the left over waves that are often perfect for high performance stand up surfing but are less desirable for traditional lay down surfers.

LOCKING UP THE GRABBER

Stand up paddle surfers have the ability to go straight to the lineup, out-position everyone, and grab all the best waves. If you know that you are, by nature, an aggressive surfer, it's time to lock up the "grabber" in you.

If you get tempted to grab every set wave that comes through, don't do it! In my opinion, the best surfers in the world are just as stoked to give a beautiful wave to someone else as he or she would be riding that wave.

Let the waves pass. Hoot and holler for other surfers and call out the incoming waves. With your high vantage point, you'll see them approaching before anyone else. When you do this, you'll make everyone's session more enjoyable.

THE CALIFORNIA TAKE-OFF

In Hawaii there's something that's affectionately called a California Take-Off. We all know that the guy up and riding closest to the breaking wave has right of way.

Well, a California Take-Off is when there's a guy who's been patiently waiting for his set wave, and while he's turning to prepare to catch the wave he was waiting for, another surfer paddles around him, out-positioning the guy, and taking his wave. While that may be acceptable in surf competition, there's no need for aggressive jockeying for position in a regular lineup.

Good things come to those who wait.

RESPECTING THE LOCALS

Above all, respect the locals. If you are a traveling surfer, remember to give first priority to the surfers who were born and raised in the area and who have chosen to make their home nearby.

Although you may be on a trip with a narrow window of opportunity for catching waves, give priority to those who live in the area and have made the ocean a part of their lives. Talk with the other surfers and find out the rules and pecking order for the area you are venturing out to surf in. While back home, dropping in either behind or in-front of another surfer may be acceptable; elsewhere it may be highly frowned upon.

THE WRAP UP

To wrap up the last few sections, as you are learning the guidelines for safe stand up paddle surfing, try surfing at the breaks where you won't have to worry about managing the crowd or dropping in on anyone. You'll be able to enjoy yourself and learn in a relaxed setting. As you venture out, you may find a new favorite wave that doesn't appeal to anyone but you.

Before each session, mentally review the rules of safety and etiquette. While you're watching from the beach before your paddle out, visualize where you'll be when you're in the water. Take note of potential hazards and decide what you'll do to avoid them.

As you follow these rules of safety and etiquette you'll be charging with the best and bringing good vibes and plenty of stoke to any lineup.

Section II.
FITNESS INTRO

FITNESS TO THE CORE

Stand up paddle surfing is an excellent core workout whether you are riding waves or flat water paddling. The sport conditions your arms, legs, abdominal muscles, back, feet, and neck to all work together in fluid harmony.

While you don't need to be incredibly coordinated, nor in top physical shape to learn to paddle surf, consistent training and paddling will raise your level of performance. Now, I'm not the most fit person on earth, but in the past, I've been an avid weightlifter, prone-paddle surfer, snowboarder, and rock climber, and as of yet, as wife says she's never seen me in as good of shape as I've been in since I started stand up paddle surfing. The health aspects of the sport are phenomenal.

As with any activity there are specific muscle groups that need to be developed before you're able to perform with the grace and power of those more seasoned in the sport. The good news is, with a little training and practice you'll be charging in no time.

The best thing you can do when you're first starting out is to paddle, paddle, paddle, and focus on proper form. You'll hear it over and over again from the best stand up paddle surfers in the world: Paddle to the pier and back; paddle to a buoy and back; paddle up and down the coast; paddle in circles around the bay. Set goals for time and distance, and keep paddling.

I remember looking out at seasoned stand up paddlers when I was first starting out, and wondering if I'd ever be able to feel as stable on my feet as they appeared to be. They told me to just keep at it. I did and soon enough the stability came.

After each paddle out, you'll be paddling and surfing with increased power, grace, and stability. Most people experience noticeable progress each and every time they paddle out. With consistent training you may soon find yourself progressing so quickly that you'll be looking to upgrade from the board you *used to* consider tippy to a more aggressive high-performance model.

For exercises you can do at home to train for stand up paddling when you can't make it to the beach visit the Appendix in the back of this book just before the Glossary.

FINE TUNING YOUR BALANCE

One of the quickest ways to speed up your learning curve and fine tune your balance is by sinking the tail so the nose of your board pops out of the water and paddling the board around and around in circles. This is called a kick turn. It's used all the time in the surf. Do this repeatedly until you can spin the board around quickly and in control.

Slide your back foot to the tail keeping your front foot firmly planted about half way up the board. With your arms outstretched and your weight forward, sink the tail, plant your paddle in the water, and with drawn out swooping strokes on one side, see how many complete circles you can do in a row before losing your balance.

Once you get comfortable with that, sink the tail even deeper and try it again. Keep track of how many strokes it takes for you to make a complete turn. Eventually you'll be able to turn the board 180° with one sweeping stroke.

A great time to work on this is when you're in the channel or outside the lineup or taking a break after a flat water paddle. Onlookers may wonder what in the world you are doing paddling in circles until you fall off, but who cares? Don't worry about it. The smile on your face will show them you're having a good time and they'll smile along with you.

Section III.
WAVE WATCH

THE WAVE

Big or small waves will work for stand up paddle surfing; it's just a matter of personal preference.

It was once thought that the sport was limited to easy rolling waves. That theory has been shattered to pieces around the globe. With the equipment available today, even the biggest bombs and hollow waves are fair game for paddle surfers.

Do you need to charge the biggest and baddest waves possible to get a thrill out of stand up paddle surfing? Not at all! You can have the time of your life on 6 inch summertime fin scraping waves.

Actually, most of the paddle surfers I know would rather spend all day on snappy knee-high waves than to battle the crowds for hours for one overhead bomb.

Beach breaks, point breaks, and reef breaks all have potential for tons of fun. Let's take a look at all of them.

BEACH BREAKS

Beach breaks form when ocean swells approach the beach and are pushed up by sandbars on the ocean floor. Beach breaks can be gentle rolling waves on small days and they can also create overhead barrels on days when the surf is really pumping.

Lazy beach breaks are often easy waves to learn on. At beach breaks, you generally don't have to worry about rocks or reef beneath the surface; however, it's a good idea to check with the locals or lifeguards as there may be unseen hazards such as piers or pilings that you should be aware of before entering the water.

In areas with beach breaks, your biggest challenge may be getting past the whitewater and out to the lineup. And, when the waves are big, be prepared for strong rip currents, punishing shorebreak, and plenty of sand in your sinuses.

POINT BREAKS

A point break is formed when an approaching swell refracts off rocks or a jetty that sticks out into the ocean. The incoming swells hit the point and then bend into shallower water forming beautiful lefts or rights depending on the swell direction and contour of the ocean floor.

Clean point breaks are the dream wave for many surfers since they lend themselves well to high performance surfing. On a good day of point break surf, you'll see plenty of snaps off the top, steep drops, and barrels. Many world class surf destinations are point breaks.

Point breaks can be a lot of fun and usually have a nice channel for easy paddling out to the lineup.

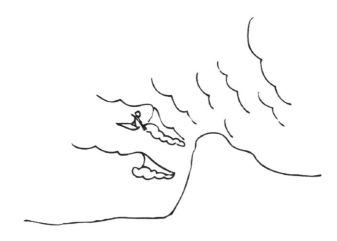

REEF VERSUS SAND

While there will always be exceptions, in general, waves that break over reef are thicker and more powerful than those that break over sand.

Waves form as the water comes in from the ocean and abruptly hit the shallow reef forcing the water up and forward to create a powerful, steep and rideable wave.

Be aware of shallow reef beneath the surface. A wipeout in the wrong place could send you home with some bloody scrapes affectionately known as reef-rash. For this reason, waves that break over the reef are not usually an ideal starting place for beginners.

Waves that break over sand are usually more sloping and forgiving. When the swells hit an underwater sandbar, instead of a sharp upward push, the wave gradually forms resulting in a mellower wave.

THE PERFECT WAVE

If you want to know what the perfect wave is for you, try this . . . Close your eyes and imagine yourself spending all day riding waves under blue skies on glassy, crystal clear, water. It's just you and two or three of your friends. You are completely stoked and the day seems like it's never going to end. Wave after wave keeps coming through, each ride more epic than the last.

Okay, do you see the wave? Can you visualize yourself on it? That's the perfect wave for your stand up paddle surf session. Keep hunting, and one day you'll find yourself riding that wave.

Section IV.
GEARING UP FOR SURF

UNDERSTANDING HOW YOUR BOARD WORKS

If it isn't the waves on a surfer's mind, it's the boards, visions of shiny new surfboards... no nicks... no dings . . . and a brand new set of fins.

It's true, there are some surfers with enough skill to surf an ironing board and make it look good. However, most of us could use the help of something a little more specialized for the sport.

The evolution of stand up paddle board design has developed so quickly that now killer board designs are available for all styles of stand up paddle surfing. The knowledge of longboard, short board, tandem, and tow-in surfboard design has culminated in a synergy of design genius for stand up paddle surfers. These boards are specialized to keep you stoked in a variety of surf conditions. So, which board is right for you? Let's have a look.

First off, be honest with yourself when you venture out to buy your first board. If you consider yourself a surfer who is super determined, not easily discouraged, who feels a drive to ride the waves, you may want to go for a more performance model.

If you fall into this category, be prepared for a more intense, crash course style learning experience. On the other hand, if you just want things nice and stable from the very beginning, get a big board and take it one step at a time.

VIRTUAL TRAINING WHEELS

If you decide to go with the performance shape for your first board, put some big fins on it until you get the hang of it. The biggest fins you can find will keep it stable and paddling straight while you're learning. Then, as you develop your ability to control the board, put some smaller fins on your board for increased maneuverability and snappy turns. It'll be sort of like removing the training wheels from your first bicycle.

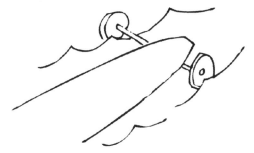

The stability of a board comes from its width and volume more than its length. Most people learn on a supertanker (super thick, super wide, and super stable). A board like this will get you up and paddling on your first day. You can never go too long or too wide on your first board, though you may need an extra hand carrying it to the beach.

Okay, you want dimensions. Well, here you go: Typical dimensions for an entry level stand up paddle surfboard are about 11 to 12 feet long, 29 to 32 inches wide and about 4 to 5 inches thick. A board like this will take you almost anywhere you want to go in the flat water.

61

Lightweight paddlers and women less than about 165 pounds may have a tough time with such a big board. Fortunately, my wife wrote the very next section about board size for women.

If you decide to go with a bigger board, be aware that an upgrade may be on the horizon for you. As you start catching more waves, you may want to switch to a smaller, more maneuverable board. It will all depend on your surfing style and personal preference.

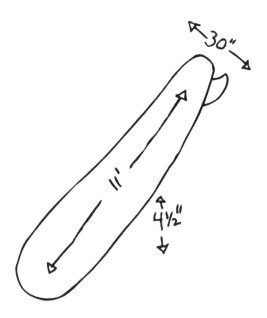

Who knows? You may fall in love with your first board and never want anything else. The fortunate thing is, stand up paddle surfboards are quite durable and hold their value well, so reselling it to raise cash for a new one shouldn't be a chore.

Now, think back to the earlier section of this book when you closed your eyes and imagined yourself riding the perfect wave. Can you tell what kind of board you were riding in that vision of mind-surfing bliss? If so, go get that board! You'll be happy about it.

To guide you along, here are some things that you might want to consider or ask about while talking with a shaper or surf shop when it's time to go shopping for your new board. You may actually want to talk to several different shapers since they each will probably have their own theories and opinions about surfboard design.

BOARD SIZE & MANAGEABILITY FOR WOMEN

My wonderful, intelligent, wise, kind, happy, beautiful, witty, glowing, lovely, skilled, smart, amazing, wave-charging wife is way more qualified than me to talk about board size and manageability for women, so this section was totally written by her (including this little paragraph to start it all off right).

In many sports, most of the equipment is usually sized for men. Alas, so is the case with stand up paddle boards. A woman of average frame and weighing less than 160lb and may find riding a "man-sized" board less manageable. A board sized for a woman should be suited to her frame, weight, and strength.

As women's shoulders are generally less broad than men's, it makes sense that the width of the board should be less as well. If you are on a board that's too wide for you, it is easy to ding the rails and difficult to paddle straight. Furthermore, to have a proper stroke with a man-size board, you need to stretch your arms further than what is comfortable, potentially causing pain to your muscles and tendons.

In the surf, a woman will find a smaller board responds much easier and quicker than a man's board. As a "lightweight" myself (5'5, 113lbs), when I take a larger board into the surf, I find it difficult to put enough weight on the tail or the rails to make the board turn how I would like. I can only put down 113lb on the tail or rail, no matter how hard I push!

Boards also come in varying weights depending on the materials used to make it. Keep this in mind when choosing a board. When you're shopping for a new board, walk it around the shop a bit before breaking out your credit card. Built-in or stick-on board handles are a girl's best friend.

Also, keep in mind that the board is going to weigh more with a wet deck pad and fins. You won't want it to be a chore to bring it down to the shore!

For surfing, most women can get away with a board 8'6" to 10" long, about 4" thick, and 27" wide. A smaller board does mean less stability, but women tend to naturally have more balance than men.

Boards like this are not as easy to find, but worth the hunt. If you can't find one from your favorite stand up paddle company, tell them they need some women's models. And, you can always get a custom board done from a local shaper.

NOSE ROCKER

"Nose rocker" refers to the amount of upward curvature in the nose of the board. In other words, a board with more rocker will have more of a banana shape to it in the front. High-performance boards have extra rocker in the nose to prevent the board from "pearling" on steep takeoffs.

Pearling is when the nose of your board sinks under the water often resulting in you flying over the front, wiping out, and diving for pearls. It's not a big deal on your average wave, but on the big ones, some extra nose rocker is necessary to avoid getting a salt water sinus cleansing after a critical takeoff.

Boards with less nose rocker often result in more glide in the flat water and make earlier entry in the waves possible. These boards are straight and they can be tons of fun. With a little kick in the tail (tail rocker), your straight board could be the perfect stand up paddle noserider for your local conditions.

If you decide to go with a performance shape, be prepared to exert some extra effort paddling in the flat water and when taking off on waves. A downside is that extra nose rocker tends to push water more than gliding over it. Some shapers have compensated for this by scooping out the nose a little to help channel the water under the board. What's best for you really depends on your local conditions and style of surfing.

If you are surfing easy rolling California, Malibu-style waves, you'll probably want less nose rocker so you can walk the board to the nose and tail, drawing smooth classic lines across the face of the wave. On the other hand, if you're charging Hawaiian style waves that are steep and powerful, some extra nose rocker is a must. When waves come up fast and early entry is not possible, you'll need to take a late drop with enough nose rocker to keep the front of your board above the water.

BOARD THICKNESS

For board thickness, four to five inches is a good rule of thumb but factors such as foam density and construction could alter that. If you are planning on buying a molded board or commercially produced shape, see if you can rent or demo the board before you buy it. This way you'll know if the board thickness is a good match for your weight and height.

Most smaller high performance boards under 10' tend to be somewhere in the range of 4 1/4" thick.

Longer high-performance shapes for bigger surfers or those who simply prefer a longer board, generally fall somewhere in the 4 1/2" - 4 5/8" thick, while "big boy" boards usually fall in the 5" – 5 ½" range for thickness.

Remember thickness doesn't always translate into stability. A board that's too thick for you will elevate you higher above the surface of the water, raising your center of gravity and possibly making everything more tippy.

I think this board is too big for me.

You'll want to have enough thickness to keep the board gliding above water with you on it, and at the same time be thin enough that you will be able to control the board in the surf.

When you stand on the board in the water, most recreational paddlers look for about one to two inches of clearance from the surface of the water up to the deck of the board.

However, I should also let you know that there are some stand up paddle surfers who prefer the deck of the board to be almost completely submerged in the flat water. They feel that less volume gives them more control on the wave. With those boards, it's slow goings paddling around the harbor but, again, it's a matter of personal preference.

If you are getting a custom board shaped just for you to use primarily in the surf, your shaper will probably build you a "one stick quiver" that is thick enough to keep you floating about 1" to 1 1/2" above the water, yet still allows for good control in the surf.

THE ONE STICK QUIVER

Just like an archer has a quiver of arrows on his back, a surfer has a quiver of boards in his garage for a variety of conditions: little ones for small waves and performance surfing, long narrow ones for big wave survival, and medium sized boards for fun days on the water. A board considered to be a "one stick quiver" is a board that combines the best elements of many boards. The goal of a one stick quiver board is that it can be used in a variety of wave conditions and can replace some of the boards that would normally make up your complete board quiver.

BOTTOM CONTOUR

The bottom contour of your board will have a huge impact on how your board performs both in the surf and the flat water. Bottom contour refers to the concave or convex properties of the bottom of the board.

To understand the bottom contour of a board, find a long measuring stick or a straight piece of wood. The flip the board upside down and place the measuring stick horizontally across the bottom of the board. In doing this, you will be able to see clearly, the bottom contour of the board from one rail to the other.

Next, with the stick placed horizontally across the bottom of the board, slide it from the nose to the tail of the board. You will be surprised at how much the contour changes on a board that may look simply flat at a distance.

In general, a board with a flat bottom will be stable with a fair amount of glide. "Vee" bottoms taper from the center of the board toward the edges. They are a little more tippy side to side but may aid with rail to rail transitions in the surf, turning in the waves, and generating speed as you travel across the face of the wave.

Many shapers are also experimenting with channels and double-barreled concaves near the tail end of the board. Really, it's a never-ending quest for the perfect board, that one you will call "magic".

A slight concave on the underside of the nose is an extremely common feature seen on most regular longboards. The concave channels water under the board to the sides and through to the fins creating stability and speed, especially when noseriding.

Depending on how that water is channeled, your board could be loose and nimble or stiff and straight. That's where the master shaper's skilled hands prove themselves.

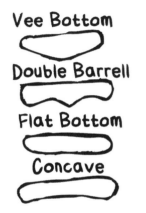

(Board Cross Sections)

Vee Bottom

Double Barrell

Flat Bottom

Concave

Even the seemingly imperceptible alteration of a board's bottom contour can make a phenomenal difference in how it travels through the water.

Add a little vee combined with some double barrel concave, a little scoop in the nose, some flat areas through the middle and *abracadabra!*, you may have a new model that performs like a dream in your local conditions.

HARD & SOFT RAILS

When you hear surfers talk about rails, they are referring to the edge around the perimeter of the board. Rails are key because, like the fins, they are in constant contact with the wave. When surfers speak of hard or soft rails, they are not talking about the durability of the construction, rather how sharp the edges are.

On a powerful turn, the nose and mid-section of the board may come free from the water, but the rails, especially near the tail, remain in constant contact with the water.

In general, you'll probably want the rails turned down more than you would on a traditional longboard. This means that the rails have more edge to them, especially near the tail. These turned down rails are also referred to as "hard" rails.

Board Cross Sections

Soft Rails   Hard Rails

Hard rails will help the board respond more quickly as well as help you paddle straight in flat water. 50/50 rails, which don't have any edge on them, may present a challenge for the stand up paddle surfer since the board may excessively drift from side to side when you are paddling around and catching waves.

If you are a more performance type surfer, harder rails will enable you to crank powerful bottom turns and snaps off the top but will require more skill to control. On the flip side, if you are looking for a pure-bred noserider style board that is forgiving in the surf, you'll probably want to get a board with softer rails.

THE DECK

The deck is the top part of the surfboard that you stand on. All decks are either flat, concave, or convex. Let's take a closer look at the pros and cons of each.

A flat deck will feel stable and will be easy on your joints and muscles. It will put your legs and feet in a natural standing position. Balancing on a big, wide board with a flat deck is as easy as standing around eating pizza. You can't go wrong with a flat deck (or a good pizza).

Some boards are built with slightly concave decks. Most flat water racing boards feature this, as do some stand up paddle surfboards. A slightly concave deck may give the rider additional leverage in the surf when pushing off the rail to make a turn. If you have trouble getting your board on edge, to turn, a slightly recessed or concave deck may be just the thing you need to get more drive out of your turns.

Additionally, a concave deck lowers the surfer's center of gravity closer to the water thus increasing how stable the board feels to the rider. Although bending your knees will also help get you closer to the water, lowering the deck a little could be the missing link for your surf style and ability.

Depending how pronounced the concave is, this type of deck may cause your knees to bend in slightly. For some paddlers, this could be a good thing.

One of the difficulties that some stand up paddlers have is being able to stay loose so as to have enough spring in their knees to absorb the bumps and chop that the ocean delivers. Stiff stand up paddlers tend to bend a lot at their waists and are constantly off balance.

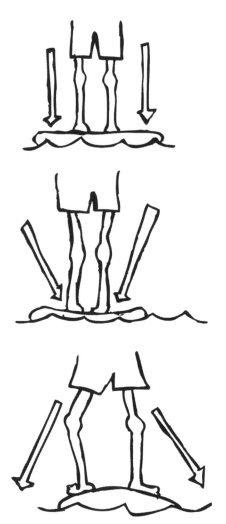

If your knees are bent in slightly, you are forced to lower your center of gravity a little. Furthermore, it focuses your balance toward the centerline of the board. The result is more stability and a greater ability to absorb the bumps with good form.

If the top of the surfboard is convex, round, or domed, as is the case with most old tandem surfboards and traditional longboards, your feet will tend to slide toward the rails of the board forcing your ankle and knee joints toward the edges of the board and into unnatural positions.

Over time, this may result in fatigue and joint discomfort. Domed decks are usually more difficult for stand up paddlers to manage since by design, they tend to slide the paddler over the side into the water.

When all is said and done, you can't go wrong with a flat deck since it calls on the muscles that you normally use in your day to day activities.

TAIL ROCKER

Just like the nose, the tail should have some slight upward curve to it. Tail rocker aids in both noseriding and performance surfing off the tail. Without any tail rocker the board will be a straight shooter: difficult and slow to turn. All boards need tail rocker.

Tail rocker is essential to nose riding. As the water wraps around the tail of the board, it will tend to force the nose up slightly and will anchor the tail of the board in the wave. This will allow you to run up to the nose to push it down and start sailing across the face of the wave with 10 toes dangling over the front.

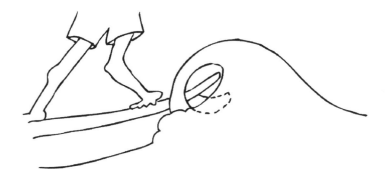

If the tail were completely straight, you could get up on the nose but if you were to hang out too long, the tail of your board would begin to slip out of the wave behind you and you'd have to do another bottom turn to set up your next walk up to the first class section of your board.

A totally straight tail will dig into the wave when you make your turn, sucking your momentum and leaving you stalled and out of gas at the bottom of the wave just before the whitewater mows you down. With some nice tail rocker, you'll initiate your turns, and instead of pushing water through your turns, you'll be able to carry the speed right into your next turn.

If the rocker of the tail matches the curvature of the wave, there will be less turbulence as your complete your turns and race across the face of the wave.

In short, no matter what conditions you paddle out in, and regardless of your surf style, some upward curve in the tail will aid you in long noserides and powerful high performance turns.

A VARIETY oF TAIL SHAPES

Tail shapes include rounded pin, square, squash, fish, diamond, swallow, and others. As it is the exit point for the water after passing under the board, tail shape has a huge impact on how stand up paddle surfboards perform.

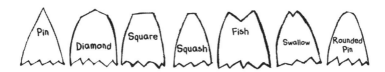

In general, squash and square tails are fun in a variety of conditions. Turns with squash and square tails are more, well, square and angular. On shorter performance boards, they throw water off the top of the wave when you do a slashing turn off the lip of the wave.

A diamond or a rounded pin will cause the board to be less stable on flat water but it'll be smooth, fast and dreamy on powerful waves. More rounded tails crank out smooth and even lines while speeding over the chop.

If you anticipate needing more speed down the line for big or hollow waves, you probably want a narrow pin tail to help you maintain speed to make the sections. You will also find some big wave boards with small swallow tails.

Fish and swallow tails create two points for the water to flow off. On a wider board, some think this makes for a smoother ride because it gives the water coming off the tail a definite direction, as opposed to a square or squash that may send the water out the back with some turbulence.

If you can, try out several boards before committing to a particular design. Even if you are going to get a custom board shaped especially for you, after trying out various designs, you will quickly recognize what features you like most and what features will be best for your style of surfing.

Still can't decide? You can never go wrong with a traditional squash tail; it's a great all around tail design that has been proven in a wide range of conditions.

BOARD CONSTRUCTION

Hand-Shaped EPS Epoxy: Many of the stand up paddle surfboards you see in the water are hand-shaped EPS epoxy. EPS stands for "expanded polystyrene". It is currently the standard construction for stand up boards and can be custom shaped to match your weight and surfing ability.

These boards are hand-shaped from foam and covered with fiberglass cloth, the same way surfboards have been produced for years. The only difference is that an epoxy resin is used to seal the board instead of the traditional polyester resin normally used for regular lay-down-paddle surfboards.

The foam core is a closed-cell foam similar to the material of those white foam drink coolers you get at the grocery store. Oversized blocks of closed cell foam used in this method of board building are readily available to shapers, making it an easy, low cost choice for custom shaping.

On a side note, although the foam is closed cell, it does not mean that the foam won't absorb water if you get a ding from hitting rocks or whacking it with your paddle. With some foam cores, water can seep between the foam beads and can be near impossible to dry out.

Additionally, if your shaper is using a high quality, high density foam, the board should absorb very little water if the board is accidentally punctured. This is a big plus especially with the edge of your paddle almost grazing the board with every stroke.

The density of EPS foam is measured in pounds (lbs). One-pound foam is lightweight and less dense. Two-pound foam is very dense and strong but heavier. One-and-a-half pound foam is the medium density foam most boards are made of.

Since EPS epoxy is lighter and more buoyant than traditional polyester surfboard blanks, even the biggest of the big boys and the smallest of the ladies can get a stand up paddle surfboard custom-built for their weight and style of surfing while keeping the board lightweight and durable.

In short, hand shaped EPS epoxy construction is the general construction of custom stand up paddle surfboards. It's light, strong, and readily available.

Epoxy Sandwich Construction: Although materials may be similar for most boards, it is a labor intensive process to build a board from start to finish. The board needs to be rough cut, shaped, glassed, sanded, and finished.

To help meet the demand for stand up paddle surfboards, there are several companies that are mass producing boards using the epoxy sandwich construction method or some variation of it.

This production method is often referred to as "pop-out" construction simply because, with this technique, the exact same board can be mechanically replicated over and over. Many surfers prefer these shapes because they are usually replicas of proven shapes that have been tested and deemed worthy of mass production. Although not all epoxy sandwich construction surfboards are guaranteed to be good shapes, many of them *are* proven and have been designed by top shapers for duplication.

The surfboards constructed in this manner have a reputation of being extremely durable and sometimes more affordable than other surfboards. They are often glassed and cured under high heat and/or pressure and are sometimes wrapped with a super durable skin resulting in an incredibly resilient finish. These boards are the most common boards available to rent or demo at rental locations because of their ability to take abuse and their availability.

If you're considering buying an epoxy sandwich surfboard, if possible, rent or demo one first. Since these boards aren't customized to your weight and ability, it's a good idea to paddle one out first before handing your credit card to the sales clerk.

Polyester: These boards are more expensive and harder to come by and, for most, less desirable. Polyester has been the standard surfboard construction method for traditional long and short surfboards for decades. Polyester stand up paddle surfboards are very heavy and much thicker than those of epoxy construction.

These boards flex and respond to the wave more so than epoxy constructed surfboards. Whether this is a good thing or not is debatable. Some argue that they perform better. Others will say that the flex is unwanted in a stand up board because it slows you down by flexing while you paddle.

Most polyester boards you'll see being used for stand up paddle surfing are actually old tandem boards. Sometimes you can find old tandem boards for sale for cheap. If you're just starting out, this could be an inexpensive and easy way to pick up your first board, (However, be aware that the curvature of the deck, which is common on tandem surfboards, may bother your ankle and knee joints).

Other Construction Methods: There are companies that are producing stand up surfboards using less traditional methods and materials such as carbon fiber, balsa, and wood laminate constructions. These boards are appearing in the lineups more and more frequently. Although we won't get into the experimental board building techniques in this book, they are also worth looking into.

YoU ARE BoARD SAVVY. NoW WHAT?

Now that you're board savvy, if you still have no idea what kind of board might be best for you, go to a surf shop and take out some boards to demo. If that isn't an option, talk it over with several shapers and surfers before ordering *your* board.

Each shaper will have a unique theory about surfboard design. Search out a shaper whose style matches yours and get his or her opinion. You may also want to get the opinion of more experienced stand up paddlers who have experimented and tested many of the more popular board designs out there.

Now, if you're still totally indecisive, there's always the option to just go out and pick up the cheapest board you can find, something to just get you going. An old tandem surfboard or that used windsurfer may be just the thing to get you on the water. Such equipment is often cheap or free but at the same time tends to be much less stable than equipment designed for stand up paddling. Hey, you can always sell it and upgrade later.

Just like when you were first learning how to prone paddle surf, truthfully, as long at it floats and it is stable enough for you, at first you won't care what board you're on. You'll be catching waves and having the time of your life. Then, once you feel like it's time to upgrade to a more specialized shape, you will have a better idea of what the perfect board for you might be.

Section V.
FINS AND MORE FINS

FINS CAN MAKE ALL THE DIFFERENCE

Most surfers would agree that fins are often the most overlooked part of a surfer's quiver. Shoot, I even finished writing the first draft of this book and forgot to put in the section on fins. The truth is that new fins or proper fin placement could possibly convert your super-tanker stick to a high performance ripper or vice-versa.

Getting the right fin combination is a complex science and at the same time perhaps one of the most addicting puzzles you'll ever work on. First, you have to decide between finning your board as a single fin, 2+1, thruster, twin fin, 5 fin, quad, or any other configuration you can dream up.

Then, once you find the fin setup that best suits your style, you get to experiment with fin height, rake, base length, foil, flex, construction, and positioning. It can seem like a daunting task at first. However when you find that perfect fin arrangement, it'll be well worth the effort.

The truth is, when we pick up a new board, we often automatically assume that the stock fins that come with the board are the best fins for the board. The reality is, those fins are sometimes just the cheapest ones that the company could get in bulk, or the fins that the shaper or CEO of the company likes on his board.

Don't get me wrong, the stock fins could be the magic setup for you, but your surfing style is unique to you and altering the setup could transform an old board into a magic stick. Let's go over the basic fins setups, and then let's test them out.

Traditional   Cutaway   Thruster   Hatchet

THE SINGLE FIN SETUP

The single fin is the original surfboard fin setup. It's versatile, fast, simple, and with the right board design can be used in everything from waves that barely break to Hawaiian-sized bombs.

The single fins setup is just that: one fin. If your board has side fins, you can simply remove the side fins and ride your board as a single fin as well.

A board with a single fin is controlled from off the tail of the board. Just step back to the tail, get your back foot over the fin, apply some pressure and *swoop*, you're changing the direction of your board. Smooth lines and flowing turns are what you'll most likely see trailing a board with just one fin.

Center fins come in all shapes and sizes. The average size for a single fin is 8 inches in height, give or take an inch.

A longer fin will be more stable and will hold better, while a shorter fin will turn easier on a wave. However, fin height isn't everything. The amount of surface area and how the water moves around the fin will determine its performance.

Confused by the huge wall of fins at your local surf shop? You can't go wrong with a traditional-looking surfboard fin. Once you master the shape that has been proven over time, you'll have a basic foundation to compare more innovative fin designs.

Unless your fin is permanently glassed on, you can adjust how far forward or back you place the fin in the fin box. In general, the further forward you place the fin, the quicker it will turn. Likewise, the further back you place the fin, the more it will hold its line and go straight.

I think it's safe to say that most people set their center fin between .5" and 1" from the front of the fin box, and when the surf gets big they move the fin back an inch or two.

In small waves, single fins are a dream. They are loose, forgiving, fast, and great for noseriding. Since there is only one fin in the water this setup minimizes drag and makes for fast paddling and extra glide. Surfing with just one fin allows for more water to wrap around the tail of the board, keeping you locked in the wave for extended noserides.

In big waves, a single fin can be a real performer for its down-the-line speed. On a narrower board with hard rails, a single fin setup can also deliver fluid high performance turns off the bottom and top. However, if the rails of your board are too soft, or round, the board may slip too much down the face of a steep wave. In this case, you'll probably want to add some side fins, making it a "2+1".

Single fins are a lot of fun. Personally, I think they feel like I'm surfing on a cloud or a giant marshmallow or something. In small surf, I love to put a single fin with a lot of flex on a shorter stand up paddle board for snappy fun. In medium surf, there's nothing quite like a traditional fin on a longer board for extended noserides. And for big surf, well, personally I prefer a 2+1 or thruster setup.

VERSATILE 2+1 FIN SETUP

Add some smaller side fins to your single fin setup and you have what's referred to as a 2+1 (two on the side plus one in the middle). The addition of the side fins to the center fin allows the board to grip the wall of a steeper wave and drive through more radical maneuvers while still maintaining the control and noseriding characteristics of a single fin setup.

The 2+1 has become the standard fin arrangement for both stand up paddle surfboards and most lay down paddle longboards. You'll find stand up paddlers running this setup in little ankle snappers as well as grinding hollow waves.

For the center fin, any traditional surfboard fin will do. However, when you add more total surface area to the fins on your board, the board usually stiffens up. Because of this, many stand up paddlers prefer to use what's called a "cutaway" center fin with side fins to reduce the total surface area of the fins

A "cutaway" is any traditionally shaped fin with a section of it removed. Usually a chunk of fin is removed from the base of the fin, shortening the base and loosening up the board. The board then maintains the stability and control of a single fin but opens it up to more high performance turns on steep waves since it can now more easily break away from traveling in a straight line.

As with a single fin setup, altering the position of the center fin even half an inch can make a world of difference in how your board behaves in the water.

Since the side fins are not usually angled straight ahead, they create drag while paddling in flat water. The side fins are for better surfing performance, not for flat water paddling. So if you're paddling around a lake or if you want to get as much glide as possible getting into the waves, remove the side fins and you'll reduce the drag.

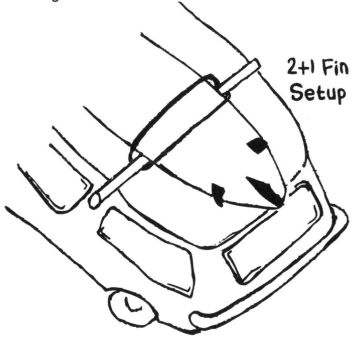

2+1 Fin Setup

In all surf conditions, you can't go wrong with a 2+1 setup. The long center fin retains the stability and control of a single fin and the side fins add the bite and hold for high performance surfing.

RoARING THRUSTER SETUPS

When all three fins are basically the same size, this is referred to as a thruster setup. This arrangement is what you'll find on most high performance shortboard surfboards and some longboard surfboards.

At the time of writing this book, the thruster is not only my personal favorite, but is the preferred setup of many professional stand up paddlers.

Most boards have side fin boxes and a long center fin for a 2+1 setup. You can convert your 2+1 board to a thruster simply with a trip to your local surf shop.

First get some thruster side fins. Most shops sell them in a pack that comes with two sides and a center fin. You'll probably have to buy the whole package of three fins but, if you have a traditional longboard center fin box like all stand up paddleboards currently have, you will only use the two side fins. The center fin that comes with the package will not fit in the center box without an adapter; and from all the feedback I've received, the adapters don't work so well.

Many stand up paddlers look for the biggest side fins they can find. It takes a lot of fin surface area to turn a lot of board and maintain that bite on the wave which keeps you in control. You don't want your board to slide out from under you in a critical spot.

Next, buy a small center fin about 3.5" to 5.00" depending on the size of your side fins and personal preference. Then, when you get home, take off your old 2+1 side fins and install the bigger thruster side fins. Also, pull out your old center fin and put your short little thruster fin in the center fin box. Slam that center fin all the way to the back of the box, closest to the tail of the board. You'll notice that the fin may even have a notch cut out of the back to allow the fin to overhang the back of the box to get it back even further. You may end up moving it forward a little, but slamming it all the way to the back is a good place to start testing.

In the flat water with a thruster setup, the board will tend to drift more while you are paddling in the flat water or paddling to catch a wave. With the fins as shallow as they are, there is less of an anchor in the water to keep you upright and paddling straight. After a few sessions you'll get used to it and it won't bother you anymore.

In the surf, a thruster fin arrangement is a performer. It carries its speed through the turns and is fast down the line. If your surf style includes a continuous series of turns and snaps, you'll probably be most at home with thrusters.

Downsides to this arrangement may include less time on the nose and less overall stability. With less fin to anchor the tail of your board in the water, the board will be more challenging to balance and your noserides may be cut shorter than you've been used to. But don't get me wrong, a skilled surfer can get plenty of tip time with thrusters. It' just takes more precise positioning and a juicy wave.

TWIN FINS, QUADS & MORE

Everyone gets the bug from time to time where they want to try something retro or experimental with their boards. I say go for it. There are plenty of surfers out there that swear that something like a twin fin, just 2 extra-large side fins, is the best setup ever for a stand up paddle surfboard, while others despise it.

There are specially designed fins to be ridden as a twin fin, so have another trip to the surf shop in order to give that arrangement a run. Twin fins usually need to be pumped down the line. A twin fin needs to constantly be turning to keep its speed. This may be just what the doctor ordered if you love taking your board rail to rail. Quads and 5 fin setups are known for being extremely quick configurations. It's all a matter of surf style and personal preference.

Let your local surf shop help you out with getting the right fins for these arrangements. Or, if you get the itch for something new, buy some fins or borrow some from one of your buddies and have fun.

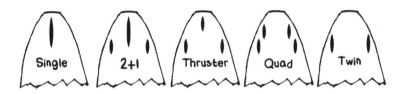

TESTING THE STOCK FINS

The stock fins that come with your board are usually a combination that performs reasonably well in a variety of conditions. They'll most likely be a 2+1 setup with side fins about 3.5" high and a center fin of about 8".

When I get a new board, I usually install the stock fins with the center fin about 1 inch back from the front of the fin box for a session or two before I start experimenting. Sometimes they're the perfect combination for the board and current conditions. How do you know if those stock fins are in just the right spot? You've got to test 'em.

Although a new set of fins isn't always as cheap as we would sometimes would hope them to be, they're definitely cheaper than a new board and will change the way your board performs in the surf. Test out the stock fins, and if they just don't feel right, try some others until you find the ultimate setup for your equipment and surf style.

SCREWING IN THE FINS

Okay, so now you've got your new board upside-down out on the front lawn. There you are, fins in hand squinting from the glare from the sun reflecting off your newly polished beauty. You screw in the side fins with the little hex screws in until they are good and snug, being aware not to over tighten them, since this could strip the threads. Now it's time to place the center fin.

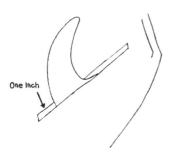

One Inch

In honesty, you'll be moving that center fin forward and back several times over the next few sessions anyway as you try to get a feel for what is right for you and the conditions you are playing in. There are some center fin screws on the market that can be adjusted by hand, making it easy to do a quick adjustment.

If the board feels like it's too stiff and it's just not turning well, try moving the center fin forward a little. If the board feels too squirrely or like it's spinning out, move the fin back some. Once you get that thing dialed in, get a marker and put a little line on your board. Then you'll know right where that baby goes next time you swap out the fins.

STARING INTO THE FIN CRYSTAL BALL

Even though I say you just pop that fin in there and forget about it, it's easier said than done. I don't think I'm alone in admitting that when I get a new fin to place, I put it in ever so carefully and gently tap it forward and back a half-millimeter at a time while staring at it from all angles as if I were gazing into the fin crystal ball to tell what the future holds for this fin placement. Of course when I get it just right, I usually realize that I forgot to put the screw plate in the box. So, I have to take it all out and start over again. Ah, good times!

ACME FIN PLACEMENT CRYSTAL BALL

Section VI.
THE BELLS & WHISTLES

ACCESSORIES

Once you finally get that perfect board picked out, it's time to round out your gear with the right accessories. Now, I'm not talking about leg warmers, shades, and sweatbands, though that could be fun; I'm talking about deck pads, leashes, etc.

The reality is the right or wrong accessories can mean the difference between a stellar session and a long swim in, especially if you're surfing outer reefs not easily accessible by others. So, let's get to it.

WHY A DECK PAD?

As soon as you have your board all picked out, the very next question you'll be asking yourself will probably be "Do I need a deck pad? If so, which one should I get?" Although most top surfers are charging the waves *with* them, it's totally up to you whether you use one or not. Personally, I recommend you *do* use a deck pad. Just to be sure, here are some of the pros and cons of each so you can make an educated decision for yourself:

Reasons to consider buying a deck pad:

1. Fewer pressure dings on the deck of your surfboard from the heels of your feet.
2. No wax means less mess and no melting.
3. It's easier on your knees when knee paddling.
4. Comfortable and easy on your feet.
5. Less fatigue for longer surf sessions.
6. Less "shifty" and more predictable than wax.

Reasons you may not want a deck pad:

1. Deck pads may retain water, adding.
2. New "feel" under your feet to get used to.
3. Longer drying time for your board.
4. May decrease power transfer from your feet.
5. Dark pads may overheat the board in the sun.
6. Additional expense.

Some surfers put patches of deck pad in the center balancing point of the board only. This provides some cushion under your feet and knees while surfing or knee paddling yet leaves the rest of the board ready to be waxed up for a traditional feel while riding waves. The challenge with this is learning to adapt to the different types of grip under your feet. One second your foot could be on a deck pad and the next on wax.

You can always try out your board with a deck pad then remove it if you don't like it. Deck pads can sometimes be a royal pain to get off but with a lot of patience and a razor blade it *can* be done. Even better would be to wax up your board and try it out with just wax before adding a deck pad. Then, if you decide a deck pad is what you need, you can just leave the board out in the sun for a bit until the wax melts, then wipe it all off.

Get your board good and clean before applying your deck pad. Any left over wax will inhibit the pad from sticking to your board securely. There are some surfboard wax remover kits that you can pick up at your local surf shop or online that are really inexpensive and well worth the cost.

A word of caution on that. Standing on a board without a deck pad will almost always create little dimples in the board called pressure dings. They don't usually affect the structural integrity of the board.

When I get a new board, I prefer to use a deck pad, but who knows; maybe I'll leave it off on my next board just to mix things up some.

There is a wide range of deck pad manufacturers out there. Their products vary by density and thickness of the pad, as well as the material used and texture. Before you jump to buy any old deck pad that's on sale, check with local stand up paddlers and find out what they're using.

I'm getting a deck paaaaaaaaaaad!

A deck pad that may be super sticky for the surf in cold water with booties could be slippery for a surfer in warm water and bare feet. When you take your stand up paddle surfboard out in the waves, the extent to which your feet are able to grip the board can make or break your session. You may be on the most advanced board ever created, but if you're slipping off when you bury the rail and crank a hard turn, you'll be swimming with the fishies.

Some surfers put a performance tail pad over the fins of their board to help them know exactly where their feet are in relation to the back of the board. Tail pads are usually heavily textured with diamond or toothed patterns for superior grip and also have a tail block to keep your foot from sliding off the back of the board.

THE RIGHT LEASH FOR SUP SURFING

A good leash is essential in flat water and surf. When you go down to your local surf shop and find yourself staring up at a wall of colorful tubing, make sure you pick out one that is strong and long.

Leashes made for big wave surfing are an excellent option because they're generally thicker, longer, and more durable than traditional leashes.

Even if you're paddling around on a lake or river, it's usually a good idea to wear a leash. Falling off a stand up paddle board is similar to falling off a skateboard: you go one way and the board goes the other. A good tug on the leash will bring the board back to you.

In calm lake conditions, you can just swim back over to your board. However, if you're in the ocean or windy conditions, a current, or a stiff gust of wind is all it takes to send your board off into the ocean faster than you can swim after it holding a paddle. So, even in on a flat ocean surface, it's a good idea to wear a leash.

Now, back to the surf where a leash is essential, not just for your safety, but for the safety of those around you. When a wave of any size swallows a stand up paddleboard, there is a tremendous amount of strain put on the leash. If the leash is old, thin, or of poor quality it'll get strung out like a piece of spaghetti. Pins, webbing, and tubing can break and you will be swimming back to the beach and collecting your board from off the rocks.

When you purchase your new board, if you ask, you can usually get a discount on a leash, and some shops will even throw one in for free. Just make sure it's a strong one.

Whatever you do, don't get a junk leash even if it's cheaper or if the store offers to sell you one at cost. It's just going to break on you endangering you and the other people in the water.

Some surf shops now also carry coiled leashes made specifically for stand up paddling. Most of these are about 10' long when fully extended and about 2' long when at rest. While there are some who choose to surf with coiled leashes, many manufacturers indicate that coiled leashes are meant for flat water paddling and not for surfing.

Straight   Coiled

A coiled leash stays out of the water eliminating drag in flat water but may get tangled and knotted after a wipeout, or could become extremely dangerous projectile if it were to break while fully extended, and quickly retract.

Spend a little extra on a quality leash. It'll last longer and help keep you, your board and everyone else in the water safe.

LEASH ANATOMY

There are two ends to a leash, the rail saver and the cuff. The cuff goes around your ankle and the rail saver fastens to the string that is attached to the leash plug on the tail of your board.

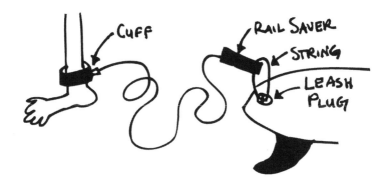

Attach the cuff to whatever foot you push with when riding a skateboard or the foot you kick a ball with. For most, it's the right foot. If your right foot is your dominant foot you are considered "regular-footed". If your left foot is dominant, you are called "goofy-footed." Either way, the cuff goes on your dominant foot.

The leash should be at least as long as your board, if not longer. This will help prevent you from getting whacked by your board in a wipeout.

It is not uncommon for a stand up board to come rocketing out of the foam after being enveloped by a wave. The buoyancy of the board will sometimes send it rocketing into the air. What goes up, must come down, and if the leash is too short, you may be headed for a crash landing on the forehead.

A while back, I experienced the board slam down in the water right next to my head twice in the same session.

Since then, I put a 10 foot leash on my 10 foot board and haven't had any similar incidents. (I'm also staying underwater a little longer before coming to the surface, which I also recommend. That could be helping to.) If you opt for a longer leash, as always, be aware of those around you. A 10 foot leash and a 10 foot board can travel a long way under the pull of a wave.

LEASH OR NO LEASH

For sure, wear a leash in the waves. I can't emphasize this enough. Leash usage is has always been a hot topic for debate. On one side of the fence you have the group of surfers that feel that leashes are for unskilled surfers and that anyone who can't control their board without a leash is a kook.

On the other side of there's the group of surfers who think the leash debate is down right silly and that safety is more important than ego.

All I know is that many of the best surfers in the world are here on the North Shore of Oahu, and you'll be hard pressed to find anyone surfing without a leash, visitor or local.

In my opinion, a lost board bouncing to the inside and hitting someone else only to send you sheepishly paddling in to help your casualty to the emergency room isn't worth any amount of macho "no-leash" attitude. I might be forever challenged on that, but when I see the kids playing in the sand and the groms surfing the inside sections, I'm willing to take some flack for it.

Section VII.
PADDLE PICKING TIME

THE PERFECT PADDLE

Paddles come in all shapes, sizes, and materials. You'll use your paddle to get you out to the lineup and into the waves as well as for steering and controlling the board while you're surfing.

There is a tremendous amount of strain put on a paddle when used by a skilled stand up paddle surfer. So, if you are serious about the sport, a high-quality paddle is in your future. Now it's time to find the perfect paddle for your needs.

Material, grip, and weight are all things to consider when buying a paddle. A paddle with too much flex may not give you the bite you need in heavier surf but may be more comfortable in small waves or flat water.

Most paddle makers offer several models that vary in materials and design. Carbon fiber, fiberglass, aluminum and wood are the most common materials used, each with its own characteristics that we'll discover in the next sections.

It is common for surf shops to have paddles available to demo or rent. After you test out several paddles you will quickly discover which paddle feels most natural to you.

After all, it's how the paddle feels to *you* that is most important. Your body is built differently than anyone else's. What feels right for someone else is not necessarily what will be best for you.

112

Most commercially produced paddles have a bent shaft just above the blade. This design was originally used in outrigger canoe paddles and has been adopted by stand up paddle makers. It allows for longer strokes and a more forward thrust.

At the beginning of the stroke, which begins toward the nose of your board, the angled blade pushes down on the water releasing the nose of your board ever so slightly from the surface tension of the water before powering though the rest of the stroke.

At the conclusion of your stroke, which ends at about your heels, with proper paddling technique, the angle of the blade allows the blade to effortlessly slip out of the water and move forward for the next stroke without lifting water.

Straight-bladed paddles may be useful for quick acceleration in the surf but could result in increased fatigue after extended paddle sessions since they tend to lift water and push down the tail of the board some at the conclusion of the stroke.

But hey, the way paddle designs are advancing, by the time you get this book, it could be that straight paddles will be considered the standard proven design. Only time and experimentation will tell.

Paddle blade shapes are generally some version of a teardrop outline. Additionally, some paddle blades have channels and specialized curvature to provide for increased control while paddling or surfing. Distance paddlers usually prefer a wider blade for touring, while those who primarily ride the surf generally prefer a narrower blade.

Like a car in first gear, a smaller blade will get you off the line fast while a larger blade will keep you cruising at a sustained speed.

DRIVING FLAT BLADES

A traditional paddle blade has a teardrop outline and is flat or slightly scooped on the back, or power side, of the blade. With a flat blade, the resistance, or "catch" of the paddle during the stroke can be varied according to how deep you sink the blade into the water.

Your may prefer the flat blade design for the ability to alter the catch of the blade, sort of like switching gears on a bicycle. The "catch" refers to how well the paddle blade grabs the water when you stroke.

Shallow strokes with the blade sunk half way in the water will allow for a gentler stroke in mellow waters or while resting. Likewise, sinking the paddle blade completely puts more blade surface in the water, almost doubling the resistance and greatly improving the "catch" of the blade, resulting in a more powerful stroke.

114

One complaint that some have about flat blades is they feel that the blade flutters in the water. Fluttering is the term used to describe how a blade wobbles from side to side along the axis of the shaft during a stroke. Some paddlers experience fluttering with a flat paddle blade while others do not.

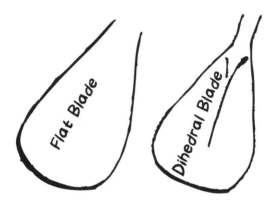

Fans of flat blades feel that they can better sense the movement of the water beneath the board and can make fine adjustments accordingly improving their stroke and control in the surf.

Many top stand up paddlers prefer a flatter blade both in flat water and surf. On the flip side, there are other top stand up paddlers who prefer what's called a dihedral blade. And that's what we're going to learn about next.

NOT THE BROOM!

Just for the record, a broomstick just won't do.

A few weeks ago I came home from an unusually good surf session and, in my frenzy of excitement, I grabbed the broom and went on to re-create my wave of the day for my wife with the use of the broom that was hanging in the kitchen.

Before I was halfway through describing the epic wave, the stick broke and I was lying on my back in the living room staring up at the ceiling with my wife standing over me laughing. Nice wave, Nate.

SMOOTH DIHEDRAL BLADES

Paddle-making companies usually offer some version of a dihedral on the power side of the paddle blade. A dihedral is basically an elevated spine that begins at the base of the shaft and tapers toward the tip of the blade on power side of the blade.

The dihedral gives direction to the water as it moves around the blade during a stroke. What does this accomplish exactly? The theory behind this is that when the water is shed evenly from the center of the blade toward the outside edges, the result is a straighter stroke with less blade fluttering.

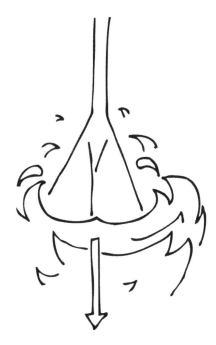

117

Less fluttering should result in a more efficient stroke. This may be a good option for beginning paddlers who have not yet developed the muscle memory for a consistent, efficient, paddle stroke. Furthermore, a straighter stroke with the help of a dihedral blade means less banging of your paddle against the rail of your board while you paddle, and thus, fewer dings to repair.

Is there a downside to a dihedral blade? Possibly. If the dihedral is too pronounced, regardless of how deep you sink the paddle blade, the catch remains the same, thus eliminating the effectiveness of sinking your blade in the water to "change gears" while paddling. Also, since the dihedral dictates how the water flows around the paddle, some feel that they lose the fine tactile sense of how the water is moving beneath the board.

In any given surf lineup you'll see paddles with flat blades and others with dihedrals each swearing that their blade is the best.

THE COVETED CARBON FIBER PADDLE

Paddle blades and shafts are made from a variety of materials each with its own unique characteristics. Carbon fiber paddles are known for being strong *and* light with a phenomenal strength to weight ratio.

Carbon paddles can usually be recognized by their dark grey or black braids. Surfers often customize these paddles with colored tape or paint to help spot the paddle in the water in the unlucky event that it is pulled from the surfer's grip during a wipeout.

Carbon fiber paddles are low maintenance, durable, and vary in construction method, quality, strength, weight, and performance. Some are constructed with carbon fiber cloth while others are built with carbon fiber strands that are spun around and around to create the shaft.

Carbon fiber threads vary in strength and stiffness so while one may feel super light and stiff, another may feel slightly heavier yet more flexible. Each paddle manufacturer uses what they feel is the ideal combination of strength, weight, and stiffness.

Most carbon fiber paddles feature a foam core in the paddle blade. This foam core combined with the air trapped in the shaft creates a buoyant paddle that floats and is easy to take out of the water at the completion of each stroke.

If you were to place a high quality paddle vertically in the water with the blade straight down and the handle up in the air, most likely, the paddle will stop sinking just after the blade is submerged. This is not an accident. At this point, the paddle is neutrally buoyant making it easier to control in the water and recover after a stroke.

Carbon fiber paddles can be ordered at the length you specify or they can usually be ordered uncut so you can decide on the paddle length on your own after you receive your paddle.

The shaft can be easily cut with a hack saw and the handle can be attached with 5-minute epoxy adhesive from your local hardware store.

FIBERGLASS PADDLES

Fiberglass paddles are also usually black in color like carbon fiber paddles. They weight slightly more than carbon fiber paddles but don't feel heavy. Fiberglass generally has more flex which is a little easier on shoulder and elbow joints.

Fiberglass paddle are also reasonably priced. They usually cost about 1/3 less than a carbon fiber paddle. Sounds like a sweet deal, huh? They are.

The downsides are they aren't quite as strong as other paddle materials, and if you're a heavier paddler, it might flex too much for you. If there's too much flex for your body build, you'll struggle to accelerate your board quickly.

WOOD PADDLES FULL OF SOUL

Wooden paddles are also strong but sport a more classic look and feel. Wooden paddles generally tend to have a bit more flex to them which may feel more natural to you. Some feel that paddles with additional flex characteristics put less strain on joints and muscles and are a good option for those recovering from injury, or that are worried about joint pain.

Wood paddles can be made from recycled wood and renewable materials making them a preferred choice for some environmentally conscious paddlers. You can even try your hand at making your own with out too much trouble.

The only downside to a wooden paddle is that a wooden paddle needs to be occasionally scanned for chips and nicks. A wood paddle that is poorly maintained will eventually absorb water and weaken if not cared for properly.

There is also the potential for unseen irregularities in the wood used which could lead to breakage. Some wood paddle makers wrap their paddles with a thin layer of fiberglass for reinforcement and ding resistance. It adds weight but also increases the paddle's durability.

INDESTRUCTIBLE ALUMINUM

A third option for paddle construction is aluminum. Aluminum paddles are less expensive to produce and are extremely strong. The trade-off is they are usually much heavier than carbon fiber or wood.

Aluminum construction may be a good option for the casual paddler looking for some bulletproof equipment or for the rare paddler whose stroke is strong enough to repeatedly break all other paddles with normal usage. Aluminum paddles are available with carbon fiber, fiberglass or molded plastic blades and are usually the most affordable option.

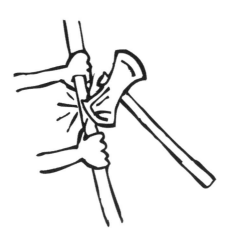

Aluminum paddles generally have more swing weight. They are a little heavier and carry more momentum with them as you stroke. Some stand up paddlers feel like they have more balance and better form when their paddle weighs more. Everyone likes something different.

Something to be aware of is that aluminum paddles are very stiff. With minimal flex, extended use of an aluminum paddle can be hard on your shoulders and joints. Unless you're breaking carbon paddles left and right, or are on a shoestring budget, I personally would recommend carbon fiber, wood, or fiberglass constructed paddle over aluminum.

INDEXED PADDLE SHAFTS

Stand up paddle shafts sometimes have what is called an indexed shaft, which is a fancy term that means the shaft is oval instead or round. In other words, if you were to look at a horizontal cross section of the paddle shaft it would be ovular instead of circular. An indexed shaft will help you to quickly get your paddle blade pointed in the right direction with one hand.

(Paddle Shaft Cross-Sections)

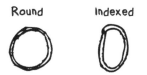

This is especially useful in the surf when you come up after a wipeout and have to start paddling right away to avoid getting hit by the next ball of whitewater. At times you may only have seconds to get one or two strokes in the right direction before the next wall hits, sending you on your second trip through the spin cycle. If you have to look down at your blade to get it facing the right direction, you may not have enough time to get any strokes in.

Some also feel that an indexed shaft gives more paddle control in normal stand up paddle surf conditions. As you experiment with paddles, you'll notice that some have the entire length of the shaft indexed, while others have only certain sections of the shaft indexed.

As you grip various paddles, you may find that a round shaft is more comfortable for you than an oval one, so give them all a try before you buy.

PADDLE HANDLE OPTIONS

The handle at the top of your paddle could make or break your paddle session. If the handle doesn't feel right, you'll spend too much time fussing with the handle instead of focusing on proper stroke, water safety and navigating the waves. There are two basic types of grip: contoured and T-grips.

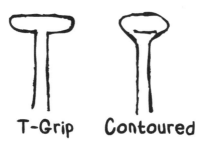

T-Grip   Contoured

Contoured grips are rounded and fit comfortably in your hand. There are no sharp edges and may be more ergonomically correct. There are pros and cons to a contoured grip.

On the upside, a contoured grip may feel more comfortable with very little potential for hot spots where blisters may form making it a good choice for extended paddle outs.

The downside of a contoured handle is that you may have less blade control in flat water or surf. When you grab the handle, basically, what you feel is what you get. Since there usually aren't many ways to wrap your fingers around it, you won't have the ability to twist the blade like can with a T-grip handle.

With a contoured handle there's a slightly greater chance for the handle to slip out of your hand, causing you to miss a stroke. However, if you wax up that handle nicely, it should stay securely in your hand.

T-grips are a more traditional shape for a paddle grip. A plus for this type of handle, as opposed to a contoured one, is that you can slide your hand up the shaft and your hand will stop at the handle every time.

With a contoured handle, there is the possibility that your hand will slide up the shaft and right off the top of the paddle. If your hand slips off the top, there's a chance you may whack yourself in the face with the paddle. How do you think I know that? Yep, it happened to me. Anyway, it's something to consider if you tend to grip your paddle loosely like I do.

FACE-WHACKED!
WAX THAT HANDLE

If only someone had a camera on the beach! It was a stormy day in head-high waves when I met my paddle face-to-face.

With a shiny contour-handled paddle in hand, I was paddling deep to get a big lumpy wave. Then, just at the point where I was going to drop down the face, the paddle slipped from my grip and whacked me square in the face. Paddle...paddle...WHACK!

Down I went with a split nose and a mark on my forehead that lasted 2 days. Man, that was a good one! Unfortunately, I was the only one around to laugh about it. Needless to say, ever since then, I'm always sure to wax my handle.

PADDLE HEIGHT

Paddle height is relatively easy to determine. The general rule of thumb for surf paddles is 6-8" over your height. A quick way for determining paddle height without a measuring tape is to spread your hand and measure from the tip of your thumb to the tip of your pinky.

Now, add that to your own personal height. That's about how long your paddle should be from the tip of the blade to the top of the handle. In Hawaii, it's called one "shaka" over your head.

If you plan on spending most of your time in the surf, you may want your paddle a little shorter, about a fist size over your head. If in doubt about your paddle length, cut the paddle a little longer and test it out.

Unfortunately there isn't a silver bullet answer for paddle height.

Everyone's arms are a different length and everyone has a different center of gravity. Something that seems to hold true is that taller, lankier, paddlers tend to prefer a paddle slightly shorter than the average length, while stockier paddlers tend to prefer their paddle slightly longer than the average length. Some paddlers that spend more time in the flat water or open ocean swells may even opt for a paddle that reaches 10" to 12" overhead.

If you order your paddle uncut, it'll arrive at your house super long with the handle detached. This way, you can cut it to whatever length you prefer. I recommend first cutting the paddle slightly longer than you think might be you ideal length. Don't glue it on yet!

First, attach the handle with a few layers of duct tape or electrical tape and take it out on the water for a few weeks. Don't worry, the handle will stay on. In fact, I've had one handle attached with duct tape for months and it has held up just fine. That way you can shorten the paddle if it feels too long.

Then, when you find the perfect length for you, simply attach the handle with some five minute epoxy from your local hardware store.

If you already epoxied the handle on and it's too long, you can gently heat up the handle with a blow dryer or heat gun to loosen up the glue and yank it off. If it's on there really good, you may have to get creative with a hack saw to make some cuts. It could be all-out paddle surgery to get that handle off. It's a pain in the neck but it can usually be done.

Once you've got the paddle cut to the right length, taped on, and you're out on the water, one indicator of correct paddle height is that the paddle should be long enough for you to casually paddle around while standing upright and also be short enough that it doesn't get caught up on the board when transferring the paddle from one side to the other, especially while riding waves.

With your knees slightly bent in a comfortable paddling position, the handle of the paddle should be about eye level mid-stroke.

As I mentioned before, stand up paddlers who spend a lot of time in the surf may cut their paddles a bit shorter because they tend to have their knees bent more while they're digging deep to paddling into waves and while they're navigating the surf.

Your center of gravity is another indicator of correct paddle height. If the paddle is too long, your center of gravity will be too high, compromising your ability to balance on the board in the surf. If this is the case, you'll feel lofty and off-balance. An excessively long paddle will also prevent you from effectively transferring power into your stroke.

On the flipside, if the paddle is too short, you'll experience muscle fatigue in your arms, legs, and back. You'll find yourself off-balance as you lean too far to one side to get the blade submersed in the water for a good stroke when it's time to dig deep, and your stroke will lack power. With some trial and error you'll discover the perfect paddle height for you.

Once you decide how long you want your paddle to be, mark it with a pencil, take a deep breath, get out the 5-minute epoxy glue, miter box, and hack saw, then do the deed.

Although epoxy tends to work great and dry in minutes for most paddles, it's a good idea to ask the paddle maker for what they recommend for attaching the handle to their paddles. They may even offer to do it for you even though you bought the paddle several weeks ago.

Section VIII.
GETTING OUT & GETTING UP

CARRYING YOUR BOARD

Okay, first things first, let's learn how to carry our boards, then let's learn how to get on and stand up. Fortunately, many boards now have handles built in but not all. Hey, if you can't get it to the water, you can't ride it.

The most common solution to getting the board to the water is to simply make someone else do it. You laugh now but you'd be surprised how many people assume the role of board and paddle caddy when their significant other takes up stand up paddling.

While your personal board-boy or board-girl may work for free for a few weeks, the time will come when you'll get an uncontrollable urge to paddle out and your breathing board carrier is not around to haul your kit to the water, and sitting in the parking lot is just not an option.

So, what's the second easiest solution? Meet up with some friends and help each other carry your boards. One grabs the tail, one grabs the nose, and off you go. You can even carry two boards at one time this way, one under each arm.

What if your friends are all at work and you've got paddle-fever? Here are a few techniques that might work for you along with some simple ratings. Here's the scale:

❖	*Desperation Move*
❖ ❖	*Sort of a Pain*
❖ ❖ ❖	*Good*
❖ ❖ ❖ ❖	*Better*
❖ ❖ ❖ ❖ ❖	*Highly Recommended*

l) The Head Balance

Rating: ❖ ❖ - *Sort of a Pain*

With the paddle in one hand, heave the board up on your head, get it balanced, and walk it to the water with everything up on top.

The nice thing about this is you're born with everything you need to get your board to the water with this technique.

The tough thing is it's really hard to keep your cool and look relaxed when you've got a big, heavy board on your head, especially if the wind is blowing.

A little side note on the head balance: I was using this board carrying technique for a while until one day when I was styling my hair after a shower with the old "shake-it-out-and-smooth-it with-your-hand" technique, well, I noticed that the top wasn't smoothing so well.

In confusion and with reluctance, I resorted to pulling out that dusty comb that was hidden in the depths of the medicine cabinet to try and fix my cranial glamour problem. What happened and what how does my hairdo problem have to do with all this?

Well, the repeated balancing act had been wearing away at the hair on the top of my head leaving scraggly uneven little hairs that were forming a lovely little bird nest up there.

The reality of this set in when people started to notice my fancy hairdo. At first I thought it was kind of cool, thinking something like, "Yeah, my hair's kind of messed up because I carry my board up there so much." Then, as it got worse, my thoughts changed to, "Yes, I did shower today. No, that's not bed-head. I'm trying to grow it back out."

2) The Shoulder Carry
Rating: ❖❖❖❖❖ - *Highly Recommended*

Heave the board up on your arm so it's leaning against your shoulder. If the wind is calm, you can balance the board with one hand and carry your paddle with the other. If the wind is blowing, you may need to use both hands to stabilize the board.

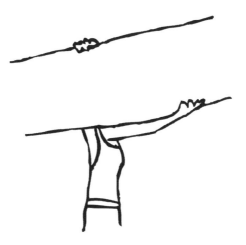

When you can get your board up on your shoulder, the weight of your board is carried by some of your strongest muscle groups: shoulders, back, and legs. Also, if you get tired, you can rest your shoulder without stopping your march to the water by pushing the board up on your head for a minute or two, and then resting it down on the other shoulder.

With a little practice you can manage your shouldered board in the wind quite well. The wind catches the board a little, but not as much as you'd think. Since the board is slightly angled as it rests against your shoulder, the wind tends to flow around it without much resistance.

Be aware of the massive blind spot on whatever side you're carrying the board on. Before changing lanes on the sidewalk or crossing the road, you'll have to lift up the board a little and peek under it, or push it up on your head to look both ways before proceeding.

If you're feeling macho and want to impress your boyfriend or girlfriend, or if you have two boards and are simply too lazy to make two trips, you can even strap two boards together and heave them both up on your shoulder at the same time and carry them to the beach.

What about the paddle? If the wind isn't too strong, you can hold the board on your shoulder with one hand, and hold the paddle in the other. If the wind *is* blowing strong, I usually just put the paddle in the hand that is holding the rail closest to the ground.

3) Nose Grab, Tail Drag
Rating: ❖❖ - Sort of a Pain

Grab your board by the nose or tail with one hand, and with your paddle in the other, let the other end drag through the sand down to the water's edge.

The nice thing about moving your board this way is it's down right easy. No need to balance the board or even carry all its weight. The wind isn't going to blow it around. And, you'll leave a nice trough in the sand that's a perfect drainage ditch for the moat around your sandcastle.

If the sand is smooth and you know where the rocks are, go ahead and drag it to the water. You'll get some minor surface scratches and wear and tear but you won't lose your balance trying to walk in the sand with your board up in the air.

However, if there are rocks beneath the surface, and your board finds one, you'll be stuck doing ding

repair for a couple days. For this reason alone, the
Nose Grab, Tail Drag gets the Sort-of-a-Pain rating.

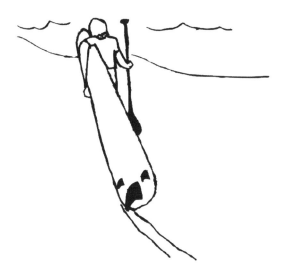

4) Hooks and Straps

Rating: ❖❖❖ - *Good*

There are various types of commercially produced
hooks and straps on the market made specifically for
carrying your board and paddle to the beach. With a
quick search on the internet or a trip to your local surf
shop, you'll easily discover several of these products.
They are usually very affordable and can be a life
saver, especially if you have quite a distance to cover
on foot or if you're not up to carrying your board on your
shoulder or head.

These products are commercially produced
solutions and most are really pretty good. I have used
several types of board carrying equipment and they all
shine in different ways.

The downsides to board carrying tools are: 1) you have to buy it and 2) you have to put it somewhere after you use it. Of course you could always bury it in the sand, throw it in the bushes, leave it with a friend, or put it in backpack to take with you out on the water.

If you have a place to put them, hooks and straps are a quick, easy, and affordable way to carry your board. If you don't have a place to store it while you're out on the water, you can always run it back to your car before paddling out.

5) Adhesive Handles

Rating: ❖❖❖❖❖ - *Better*

Adhesive handles are an easy solution for board carrying. These handles attach to any board using high strength adhesives. Some people are a bit wary of trusting a handle attached by a pair of big stickers to carry their boards, but I've yet to hear of one coming unstuck.

Be sure to place the handle in the balancing part of the board while the fins are in place so that the weight is evenly distributed when you finally attach the handle.

Are there any downsides to stick-on handles? Well, it does create something to step around on the top of your board but for most people the benefits outweigh the alternatives and it's a low cost, low profile, solution to board carrying for any stand up paddle board.

BEFORE YOU PUT YOUR BOARD IN THE WATER

Before putting your board in the water, it's a good idea to stretch! I'm telling you -- whether the waves are pumping or gently rolling through, take the time to stretch out your neck, shoulders, arms, back, and legs.

About half of the injuries that I hear about go something like this, "The waves were so good, I just ran to the water and didn't even think about stretching. Then, after my first wave I pulled some muscle in my back near my ribs." Or, "It was so mellow and clean that I didn't think I needed to stretch, and while I was paddling out I pulled a muscle." Stand up paddling calls on so many little muscle groups that it is undoubtedly important to get stretched out thoroughly beforehand.

It's usually some little muscle we don't think too much about that gets strained. It's that same muscle that you pull when you're sitting at your computer and you drop a peanut on the floor, and in a valiant effort to save that lone peanut before it disappears forever in the shag carpet, you bend down and lunge for it.

Then, just as your fingertips grasp that beloved morsel of nutty goodness, trouble strikes and it sounds like this, "Oops, I dropped a peanut." *POP!* "Oh, my back!" And then you're out of commission for several days while the surf's up. And all of this could have been prevented if you had stretched before cracking open that beautiful can of mixed nuts. . . I mean before paddling out.

139

The point is, before you begin your voyage over the great watery abyss of your local pond or that big puddle we call the Pacific Ocean, stretch out everything completely, both small and major muscle groups.

You'll perform better and you'll greatly decrease your chance of injury. Now that I'm thinking about it, I better stretch a little before I dig into this bag of strawberry yogurt raisins. I'm bound to drop one the floor.

TWO WAYS TO GET ON YOUR BOARD

Now that you're all stretched out and ready to go, it's time to get wet. When you get to the water's edge, gently let the nose of your board down into the water. Walk your board out until you're about knee to waist deep before getting on. If you jump on too early, the tail will probably hit the sand or rocks below and leave you stranded with a nicked fin.

Once you're out in the water, locate the center of your board before you climb on. Hey, if you biff it on the first attempt to mount your board, it's okay. Just smile and try again. We've all been there.

Don't try and sneak up on the board from the tail. If you try and slide yourself up the tail of the board, the board is going to slip out from under you and you'll be chasing it all over the place. Like I said, locate the center of the board, and get on there.

There are two ways to get on your board once you've got it waded out in the water and have positioned yourself on the side near the center of the board.

A) Reach across and grab the opposite side of the board to counter-balance your weight. Then, bring one knee up on top of the board, and then the other.

B) Reach across and grab the opposite side of the board, then scoot yourself up over the side lying on your stomach first, then bring your knees up under you one at a time.

A handle on your board will make it way easier to get on your board, especially in deep water. Actually, some paddlers prefer to lie down and paddle with their arms like you'd paddle a normal surfboard until they get into deeper water before getting up on their knees and feet.

While you're pulling yourself up on your board, if you need 2 hands, just gently place your paddle horizontally across the nose of your board. It'll stay there. And if it slips off into the water, it'll float.

Once you're up on top and feeling stable, place your paddle crossway on top of your board and hold on to it with two hands to keep your balance. Now that you're on all fours with the paddle in hand, you're ready to stand up.

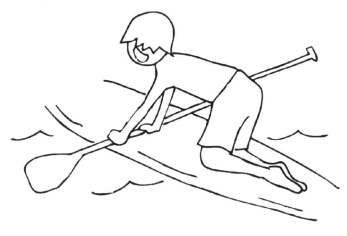

SUPER SUPPADDLE GUY

Oh yeah, now's the magic moment. It's time to add the "stand up" part to this sport we call stand up paddling. There several ways to stand up on your board. Let's cover a few of them.

If you've got a good pair of legs and want to make a name for yourself, just run to the water, slide the board in and jump up on two feet straight from the water's edge.

If successful, the beachgoers will call you something like *Super SUPaddle Guy.* If you're unsuccessful, you'll make a name for yourself like, *That Stand Up Paddler Who Biffed it on the Sand Guy.* It may make or break your career, or neck, but if you feel the risk is worth the potential fame and glory, go for it.

TWO WAYS TO EASILY STAND UP

Okay, now let's look at two conservative and controlled techniques for getting to your feet. Both of these techniques start with you on your hands and knees like a dog or a cat, with the paddle in both hands horizontally in front of you on your board just like in the next picture.

Make a quick visual check of where the center balancing point of the board is because that's where you'll be placing your feet. If your board has a handle, it's usually in the center point of the board. Once you've located approximately where that is, bring one of your feet up underneath you placing it flat on the board near the edge of the board. Keep your hands and paddle on the board in front of you and place your heel flat on the board beneath you.

Do your best to keep your heel planted firmly on your board. This will give you more stability once you're on both feet.

Next bring your other foot up under you along side the other in a nice wide stance. Then, slowly straighten your back and extend your legs just a little. Don't straighten your legs all the way. Remember to keep them slightly bent. Your feet should be about shoulder width apart or a little wider for added stability.

As soon as you're up, immediately reach out and stick your paddle in the water making sure you have one hand on top. That paddle is like the third leg of a stool. As you feel yourself tipping to one side or the other, you can catch yourself with the paddle by pushing down on the water with the blade.

Next, with your paddle in the water, extend both arms out in front of you and give a couple quick strokes to get a little forward momentum. Just like riding a bike, when you're moving it's easier to keep your balance.

Look straight ahead while you do this. While it sounds logical to look at your feet, the water, and your legs, if you look straight ahead at a stationary object like a tree, boat, bridge, or the shoreline. It will become a point of reference and help you mentally stabilize yourself. If you watch the water, it's where you're going to go.

And finally, relax. Take a deep slow breath. It'll feed oxygen to your muscles and calm your racing mind. Hey, there's a lot to think about when you're first getting started: the board, the paddle, the stance, the stroke, the posture. Once you know technically what you're supposed to do, simply relax. With a little practice, getting on and standing up will be second nature to you.

Before closing out this section, let's go over one more method to get up on your feet from a kneeling position. Just as before, locate the center line of the board between the nose and tail of the board and visualize where you will be placing your feet. Again, hold the paddle in both hands across the board in front of you.

This time, bring both feet underneath you one at a time, however, instead of putting your heels flat on the board, keep your weight on the balls of your feet and your hands. Stay in this position until you feel fairly stable. Then, when you're ready, roll your weight back onto your heels as you straighten your back upright and reach out with your arms to take your first stroke.

The Stability Checklist

There are a number of little things you can do to increase your stability on a stand up paddle board. When you're out on the water and feeling shaky on your feet, bust out this book and follow this checklist of things that will make you stable. The answer to all of these questions should be YES!

□ Am I looking ahead instead of at the water?
□ Are my knees slightly bent?
□ Can I wiggle my toes while I am standing?
□ Am I staying relaxed?
□ Do I have a nice wide stance with my feet?
□ Am I in the middle of the board?
□ Am I extending both arms out in front of me?
□ Are my feet facing forward?
□ Is my paddle the right height?
□ Is my paddle blade facing the right direction?
□ Does my board have enough buoyancy for me?
□ Am I breathing deep and slow?
□ Am I smiling?

WHITE-KNUCKLE, DEATH-GRIP TOE PAIN

White-knuckle death-grip toe pain occurs when, in an effort to gain stability on a stand up paddle board, a paddler curls his or her toes in an attempt to sink his or her non-existent talons into the top of the board.

Toe knuckles turn white, feet cramp up, and I even met one girl who dislocated her toes trying to grip the board.

Relax my friends. Sit your behind down just a little more and let your center of gravity fall between the balls of your feet and your heels. You should even be able to wiggle your toes while you're paddling. Take a deep breathe and let the stability come from your legs and core, not your toes.

A STYLISH DISMOUNT

It's inevitable that you are going to get wet but that is part of the fun so don't be nervous about taking a dip in the water. When that little alarm goes off in your head that says, "Attention all body parts! You're going to fall off this board!" just jump all the way off. If you try to stay on your board at all costs, you are more likely to put a ding or a hole in your board from whacking it with the paddle in an attempt to stay dry. Or, you may knock your knuckles, land on your knee, or the paddle might bounce off the board back at you or something.

Hey, if you're going to fall off, just go for it and do it with style. *Cannonball!*

If you're not into getting wet, you might as well pull that rowing machine out from under your bed, blow the dust off it and row your heart out in your dry bedroom. If you're on the water, you're getting wet or you're not having enough fun!

148

The best surfers in the world are where they are today because they aren't afraid to fall down. And when they fall, they get back up. It's as simple as that. Personally, I get soaked all the time, but you know what? I love every moment of it.

After a few sessions, your standing ups will quickly outnumber your falling downs and you'll be cruising.

JUST IN CASE YoU HAPPEN To FALL oFF

If by chance you happen to fall off, and cannonballs are not your thing, I thought I'd include a couple tips for taking the dive safely and with style.

Now, you may not be the "falling" type but just in case the planets misalign and your super-human reflexes get compromised by galactic dust that swoops down from the outer reaches of a neighboring solar system that happens to hit you just as the wind blows and a little wave rocks your board sending you into the water, you'll need to learn how to fall.

Tip #1: If you know you're going to fall off, embrace the moment and go with it. If you try and catch yourself on your board, you may bruise your knees, bang your knuckles, or even hit yourself with your own paddle. If the little echoing voice in your head says, "Attention. You've leaned too far. You are now going to fall off your board," just give a good times holler like, "Sheeyahoo!" Then, jump off and make a big splash.

Tip #2: Keep the paddle away from your board and others as you take your watery plunge. Paddles are relatively sharp and could put a nice water-sucking hole in your board, your friend's board, or your friend's knee-cap with a good stiff whack.

Tip #3: Give it some flair. Stand up paddling is a totally fun sport. Next time you go off, try a cannonball, belly flop, jackhammer, or your own super twisto-flexo spintastic rump dump. Whatever dismount you choose, be aware of the water depth to avoid kicking the reef or hitting bottom.

Tips #4A - 4E: (Advanced Only) For those of you who simply have to play it cool at the risk of the gang giving you a hard time, here's some things you can do to try and play it off like you meant to fall off your board.

A) After falling in, surface with your nose pointed toward the sky and confidently shake your head as if you just wanted to get your hair wet and cool off.

B) After making a splash, come out of the water with a purpose, such as, "I just wanted to swim a little." Push your paddle out in front of you and start swimming after it with your board trailing behind you.

C) When you hit the water, start swimming for the bottom as if you saw something interesting down there. Then, when you come up you can say something like, "Yeah, I though I saw a shark down there. I was just going to check it out. It's okay." Or, "Yeah, I thought I saw a surfboard fin down there on the bottom so I went down to have a look, and I wanted to get a good jump into the water so I could get down there quicker, and I saw this cool fish on the way down and almost lost sight of the, uhh . . . rock, I mean the fin, but when I got down there it was just a shell."

D) As you surface, push your board up on one side flipping it over. Then swim over to the back as if you just wanted to check out your fins and make sure they're all there and secure, and to have a look at the wear and tear on your leash plug and string. (There's got to be some damage there from that last big wave. *Wink, wink.*)

E) Just come up and tell everyone one around you in a loud voice, "I meant to do that. Hey buddy, I meant to do that. Yo, I meant to do that just now, really; for real."

Section IX.
STANCE & POSTURE

THE ESSENTIALS

Proper foot stance and posture will make a world of difference in your stand up paddle surfing experience. As in any sport, proper form is essential.

The parallel stance, staggered stance, and surf stance are all used in stand up paddle surfing. The mastery of these basic stances combined with correct posture will increase your power, confidence, ability and endurance as a paddle surfer.

CORRECT POSTURE RIGHT FROM THE START

Your posture in the flat water should be comfortable and relaxed with your head up, back straight but not stiff, and knees slightly bent. In this neutral stance you will be able to absorb the bumps in the water while paddling and surfing.

When you first start out, you may be tempted to bend at the waist when surface chop or whitewater hits. Resist the urge to bend at your waist, and try to absorb the bumps with your knees and hips with both arms extended out in front of you. You'll glide almost effortlessly over the surface chop and will soon embrace the rolling ripples of the ocean as they gently pass under you.

If you notice excessive fatigue in your legs or back, it is probably the result of improper posture. To correct this, lift your arms straight up, high above your head. Bend your knees slightly as you roll your shoulders back while bringing your hands down to your side. This will line your shoulders up with your feet, relax your muscles, and put you back in a correct neutral position. You should now feel comfortable, natural, and relaxed. Now you're ready to move to a parallel, staggered, or deep staggered stance.

THE MOST STABLE STANCE

The most common and most stable stance is the parallel stance. With correct posture and knees slightly bent, place your feet facing forward about shoulder width apart near the mid-section of the board. This is the parallel stance.

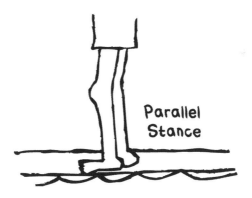

Parallel
Stance

If your feet are too far forward, the nose of the board will sink and you'll find yourself pushing water as you paddle. Likewise, if you stand too far back you'll sink the tail and again find yourself pushing water.

Once you find the balancing point of your surfboard you're all set. From the parallel stance you will be able to paddle around easily in most conditions, as well as punch through small whitewater and turn the board around to catch waves.

After finding the balancing point of the board, if you are still struggling somewhat to maintain balance, pick a stationary point on the horizon such as the waterline or shoreline and keep your eyes on it while you paddle. It will give you a point of reference and help you to keep your balance while you paddle.

If you look at your feet or the water, well, water moves and so will you. Choose a point of reference and make that your focus.

Take a deep, relaxing breath. Have a nice slow breath in and a slow one out. For some reason it magically stops legs from shaking and will help you refocus your efforts.

THE STAGGERED STANCE

The staggered stance is also done in the midsection of the board with feet facing forward. It is identical to the parallel stance with the exception of one foot slightly ahead of the other. Sometimes your back foot may feel more comfortable with your toes slightly turned outward. That back foot will be constantly changing position, so just keep it comfortable and loose for now.

With your feet slightly staggered, you will get more power and control over the board while both paddling and turning the board around. The board will be more prone to tipping from side to side, however, you will feel more stability front to back.

Staggered
Stance

When paddling long-distances, it's a good idea to switch between the parallel stance and the staggered stance to prevent fatigue and keep the blood flowing to all the muscles in your legs and feet. Try alternating which foot you put forward. At first it will feel more natural to put one ahead of the other, but with practice, you'll be able to alternate feet with ease.

The staggered stance is an excellent position to be in while paddling to catch waves of all sizes. It will give you more power in your stroke and will help you to balance as you drop down the face of a wave.

You'll probably start paddling for a wave in the parallel stance then switch to the staggered stance as you pick up speed, and finally end up in a traditional surf stance as you catch a wave.

THE SURF STANCE DANCE

The surf stance is similar to the staggered stance in that one foot is near the center, or balancing point, of the board. However, in surf stance, your back foot is dropped back closer to the tail of the board. This stance is very tippy when the board is not in motion so be sure to keep your paddle in the water and brace yourself.

This stance will help you to maintain front to back stability when taking off late on waves, punching through thick whitewater, and delivering the power needed to bury the rail for deep, driving, bottom turns and cutbacks while surfing.

You will often transition between the parallel, staggered, and surf stances in the process of stroking in, riding, and kicking out a wave. Practice transitioning between these stances during your flat water exercises.

Casually paddle along in a parallel stance then quickly transition to a staggered stance as if you were paddling to catch a wave then, drop to a surf stance briefly and quickly transition back to a parallel stance. Do this over and over again in flat water. Once you've mastered these transitions, practice with the opposite foot forward.

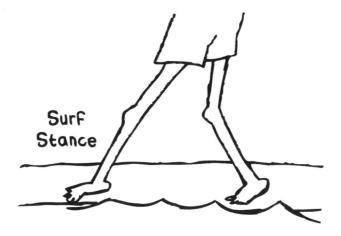

Surf
Stance

Section X.
PADDLE & BOARD CONTROL

PADDLING & TURNING LIKE A CHAMP

"They make it look so easy!" is a comment often heard coming from spectators at stand up paddle surfing events. It's true, skilled paddle surfers make it look very easy.

The fluidity and grace with which they paddle and turn their boards is almost hypnotic to the onlooker. Proper paddling and turning techniques are the keys to surfing with such finesse. Although at first, holding a paddle while surfing may seem somewhat awkward, it will soon become a natural extension of your body.

Here are some basic tricks and techniques that will put more power into your stroke, help you turn your board around with speed, and further refine your style.

As was mentioned before, the best way to refine your paddling skills after getting properly instructed is to paddle, paddle, paddle. At first you may feel a little off-balance and you may feel like you're just not getting the drive that you need in order to get into waves or to cruise effortlessly along the coast. Relax. It will come.

If you have ever watched someone learning to prone paddle surf, or if you can think back to when you first learned how to surf, play an instrument, or drive a car, you'll recall the busy, almost frantic, mindset that you had while you attempted to synchronize your thoughts and actions to produce something graceful and controlled. The same holds true for learning to stand up paddle.

Beginner lay-down paddle surfers are perfect examples. You'll notice that new surfers work harder than anyone else on the water in their effort to catch waves. They paddle their hearts out on massive boards desperately struggling to start skimming down the surface of a wave.

Conversely, on the same wave you'll often find experienced surfers on short little boards easily dropping into waves with two or three quick strokes. The experienced surfers have stronger, more efficient strokes, and they know how to read the waves, shift their weight, and maintain control. The same learning curve holds true for beginning paddle surfers. With time and practice you too will glide into the surf with ease.

GRIPPING THE PADDLE

Grip the paddle with one hand at the top of the shaft and the other about 1/3 the way down from the top. The hand grasping the handle at the top of the shaft should be in the hand opposite of the side of the board that the blade is on. If you feel like you are reaching or bending over excessively at the waist, bend your knees or slide your hand along the shaft a little until you feel that you are in a restful and neutral position.

Although it may seem counterintuitive, make sure the blade is angled so that when you raise the paddle up in front of you the blade is angled away from you and toward the nose of your board. On most paddles, the company logo on the paddle blade should be facing forward. In other words, the blade should angle forward and away from you rather than towards you.

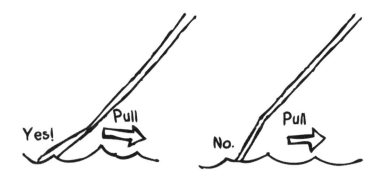

THE FORWARD STROKE

A proper forward stroke is the foundation for a successful stand up paddle experience. When your stroke is good, you'll be able to conserve energy, travel longer distances, and power yourself into the fat waves you've been dreaming of.

The stroke begins in front of you near the nose of your board and ends near the heel of your foot. To begin the standard forward stroke, bend your knees and waist slightly while reaching forward, extending both arms, and placing the blade in the water toward the nose of your board.

When the paddle enters the water, try to keep it as stationary as possible while pulling back on it. The less the blade moves as you stroke, the more efficiently you'll be able to transfer power. At the beginning of each stroke, the angled blade helps you to pull your board up and forward.

It's almost imperceptible, but when your paddle blade first hits the water, it gently releases the nose of your board from the surface tension of the water. With the nose free your stroke becomes much more effective.

After initiating a stroke, pull the blade back straight toward you, and you'll pull yourself forward and across the water. If you bend your arms while you stroke, you will be using your back and arms for power. If you keep both of your arms fairly stiff from the beginning of the stroke to the end, you will be drawing power from your core muscles which are much stronger.

Again, try and keep the blade straight and steady as you stroke so that you are able to make maximum use of the surface area of your paddle blade. If your blade tends to flutter or you find yourself banging your board with the paddle blade, use a gentler stroke and concentrate on good form. Practice makes perfect and as your muscle memory increases, you can add more power to your paddling.

If you still find yourself struggling with blade control, you may want to look into getting a paddle with a more pronounced dihedral on the power side of the blade. Have a review of the section on paddles for more information on dihedral blades.

166

After powering through the mid-section of your stroke, when the paddle blade reaches somewhere in the vicinity of your heel, release the blade from the water and reach forward to begin the next stroke. At this point, because of the angle of the blade, the paddle should come clean out of the water.

If you were to continue the stroke through toward the tail of your board, as you pull the paddle from the water you will find yourself lifting water with it. If this is the case, not only will you find yourself exerting additional energy to get the paddle out of the water, but you'll also be pushing the tail of the board down ever so slightly, creating drag.

To illustrate this, practice a stroke while you're standing in the sand. Stroke the sand as if it were water. Watch how the sand moves around your blade and take note of how you will find yourself lifting sand should you continue your stroke beyond you heels. Also, notice how at the completion of your stroke your top arm needs to be extended for the angled blade to come straight up out of the water.

If you're releasing the blade from the water at the proper time, with each stroke you will feel only one driving pull, "pull. . . pull. . . pull." If you are carrying your stroke too far behind you, or if your arms aren't properly positioned, you'll feel two pulls with each stroke, "pull-pull. . . pull-pull. . . pull-pull."

One final note on the basic stroke. As you reach forward to place the blade in the water, keep your top arm, the one holding the handle, with only a slight bend it in. Do the same with your lower arm.

As you paddle, drive the paddle down and back with your top hand and pull the blade toward you with your bottom hand. And to further engage your core muscles and generate more power, keep your arms fairly straight and stiff throughout your stroke to use your stomach and core muscles to power your stoke. Remember to keep your knees bent while you reach out to grab the water with your paddle blade.

Straight arms force you to use your core muscles. If you're arms are bent too much or if you are bending at the waist too far, your balance will be off and you'll have little or no power in your stroke. Also, paddlers who don't reach their arms out far enough often appear to be "poking and prodding" at the water with their paddle instead of planting and driving it back with power.

With proper form right from the beginning, your muscle memory will develop and all that you'll have left to do is increase in strength and speed. If you're just starting out or have to break some bad paddle habits, focus on proper form; power will come with practice.

Soon enough, you'll be paddling faster and surfing with greater control.

CAN I PADDLE STRAIGHT?

One of the greatest things about stand up paddle surfing is being amongst the ever-changing elements. As your environment changes, so will your stroke and the little techniques you'll use to keep your board paddling straight ahead.

You'll feel the wind blow from behind and you'll alter your stroke. The backwash from the beach will change the direction that the water is moving under your board and you will alter your stroke. Two waves will come at the same time from slightly different directions, and you'll alter your stroke.

On a stand up paddle board, you've got the wind, the surface chop, the under current and the waves to work around. Whichever force is strongest at any given moment will decide where you'll start drifting off to if you stop paddling. The challenge is, if the wind is blowing you one way, then it stops, the waves might start pushing you the opposite way. In a constantly changing environment, it's good to know several tricks for paddling straight.

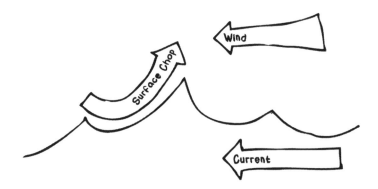

One thing you can do which creates some drag but will help you keep moving the right direction is to sink the rail of your board on the side that you are paddling on a little deeper in the water. So, if your paddle blade is on your right side, put a little extra pressure on your right foot so the rail of your board sinks in the water *just a bit* as you stroke. This engages the fins and gets them working for you as you "surf" in the flat water.

Between strokes, you may find that you get a little extra glide if you let the board flatten back out before the next stroke. Dip/stroke… glide… dip/stoke…

glide… dip/stroke… glide. Then do the same with the opposite side when you switch your paddle blade to the other side of your board.

Another tip is to be aware of where you place your paddle blade when you begin your stroke. Your stand up paddle surfboard is wider at your feet and narrower near the nose. When beginning your stroke, there is a natural inclination to reach forward, place the paddle in the water a few inches from nose of your board and pull back following the outline of the board.

Well, since your board curves in toward the nose, a stroke that you thought was straight is actually a mildly arching side sweep that may be swinging the nose of your board around.

To prevent this and paddle straighter, begin your stroke by placing your paddle about 8 to 12 inches to the side of nose of your board and finishing the stroke approximately one inch from the side of the board near your feet. Combine this with the counterbalancing of the rail we were just talking about and you'll be paddling straighter than ever!

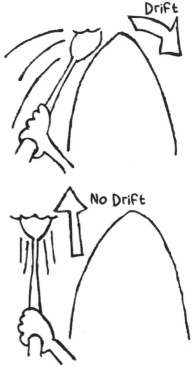

Drift

No Drift

A great way to practice paddling your board straight is to choose a landmark off in the distance and paddle straight towards it. Pay close attention to the subtle changes in direction that occur as you paddle, and do your best to correct those. Focus on keeping the nose of your board pointed at that landmark while you paddle.

Eventually you'll intuitively feel the slight direction changes and will be able to correct your course even before the wind or waves start to push you around. Stay focused, keep at it, and when you've mastered your forward stroke, pass on these tips along with some words of encouragement to others who are at the beginning of the learning curve.

THE LEFT OR RIGHT SIDE?

Both! You will paddle your board on both the left and right side as determined by the environmental conditions. If the air is still and there is no current in the water, you'll probably paddle four to six strokes on one side and then four to six on the other.

If the wind is blowing and the water is moving, you may travel to your destination paddling exclusively on one side of the board to keep from being blown off course. All that means is that you'll be paddling on the other side the whole way back. The conditions will dictate.

You may also find that you have a dominant side for paddling. There's nothing wrong with that. However, if you can paddle equally as strong on both sides, you'll catch more waves and paddle with outstanding control.

SHORT STROKES OR LONG STROKES?

Sometimes you will need to paddle with short, quick strokes and other occasions will call for longer, more drawn out strokes.

Let's compare long and short strokes to the gears on a car or bicycle. The short strokes would be equivalent to first gear and the long strokes could be compared to the tenth gear. Short strokes in "first gear" will get you quickly racing off the starting line while the long "tenth gear" strokes will carry you further with less effort.

You'll use long strokes to travel distances, conserve energy and to lazily paddle into waves when you have plenty of time to get moving before the swell reaches you.

Conversely, you'll use short explosive strokes to quickly speed up for dropping into waves, punching through whitewater, and fine tuning the direction of your board.

ONE-STROKE ONE-EIGHTIES

Next, let's discuss using the paddle to swing the nose of your board around to catch a wave. The mastery of a maneuver used to quickly spin your board around 180°, often called a "kick turn", is essential for every proficient stand up paddle surfer. We'll cover that in just a minute.

If you have a background in traditional lay-down prone-paddle surfing, you'll notice that it can take quite a bit longer to get a stand up paddle board turned into the right position for catching waves than it takes to flip over a little shortboard before an approaching set.

From your heightened vantage point, in most conditions you should be able to see the approaching waves long before it's time to turn your board around and start paddling. But, when heavy swells come barreling through, you'll need the skill to be able to spin your board around quickly to drop down the face of the wave.

As the bomb waves start rolling through, sometimes it's a matter of taking off or getting tossed. If you can't get your board turned around in time to catch the wave, you may be destined for the latter.

Here are some techniques you can practice that will help get your board turned around quickly. With practice, you'll whip your board around 180° in one controlled stroke.

SMOOTH STANDING TURNS

The standing turn is the most mellow way to turn your board around. It's slow and easy, so pick your wave and give yourself plenty of time to get turned around. In fact, this turn is so gradual that if I personally do a standing turn, I actually hear these beeping noises in the back of my head. You know those warning beeps that sound when a school bus puts the gears in reverse? Those are the ones -- "beep...beep...beep...beep." It's like, "Hello everybody! I'm turning around, make way."

Here's how it's done. With your feet in a parallel or staggered stance, place your paddle blade near the nose of your board and bring the paddle handle down to the height of your stomach. Next, in an arching "C" shaped stroke, push the paddle blade away from the nose of your board. Then, when the blade is half way through the "C" that you're drawing in the water, pull the blade in toward the tail of your board.

After this, immediately switch the paddle to the opposite side of the board and repeat the same "C" stroke pattern starting from the tail of the board and stroking up toward the nose. Repeat this a few times until you are turned around completely . . . "C" stroke forward on one side, then "C" stroke backward on the other as if you were drawing a huge circle around your board.

175

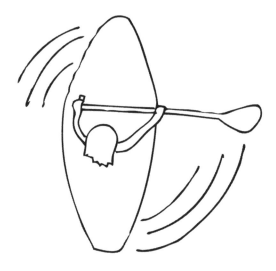

Take it easy with this turn. It's meant to be slow. If you put too much power into it, you'll put excessive twisting stress on your knees and could injure yourself. If you need to turn more quickly, stagger your feet a little more and shift your feet back toward the tail some. It'll loosen up the board and allow you to "kick turn" the board without blowing a knee cap or something.

BUSTING QUICK KICK TURNS

A kick turn is the quickest and most efficient way to turn your paddle surfboard around in any situation. A kick turn can spin the board around 180° in one sweeping stroke.

The best stand up paddlers in the world are constantly practicing their kick turns in all conditions, as it's excellent for whipping your board around to catch a wave on a moment's notice.

The method behind a kick turn is quite simple in theory. Assume a surf stance by placing your back foot above the rear fins to sink the tail as deep as possible while keeping your paddle in the water for stability. Then, with a sweeping stroke on one side, spin the board around before leveling it back out again.

With the tail submerged, your board is going to feel tippy and squirrely. Immediately stroke hard and deep on one side to swing the nose of the board around 180°. As you are practicing this technique, you can begin by turning the board around with several short, quick strokes.

Then, as your technique improves and you become more familiar with your board, you can work towards being able to turn the board completely around with just one long sweeping stroke.

After your board is turned around, shift your feet forward into a parallel or staggered stance to bring the tail back out of the water. With the kick turn complete, your board will be facing the opposite direction of where you were facing when you started your turn and you will be ready to paddle for a wave.

WAVE TAKE-OFFS IN FLAT WATER

Learning to catch waves on a stand up paddle board is considerably more challenging than learning to catch waves on a traditional lay down paddle surfboard? Why? You have to enter the wave under your own power.

Unlike when you take a regular surf lesson, where the instructor puts you on a big board and pushes you into a wave, nobody can push you into a wave on a stand up paddle board. It has to be done by person number one, that's you!

If you've got plenty of empty waves nearby where you can kook it for a while as you learn to catch waves on your stand up board, that's great. If your local lineups are always lined with people or if you want to get as proficient as possible before venturing into the surf, here's how you can simulate a take off in flat water.

Start by paddling straight at a regular pace in a parallel or staggered stance. Then, after you've got some momentum, immediately drop to a surf stance with your rear foot back on the tail of the board. Sink the tail of your board as deep as possible.

Then, reach out with your paddle blade and pull yourself out of the watery hole you just sunk the tail of your board into. As you reach forward and stroke, the buoyancy of your board, combined with the stroke of your paddle, gives a small energetic push forward and out of the water similar to how a wave accelerates you upon take off.

Repeat it over and over as you paddle along. Paddle, paddle...step back and sink tail...reach and pull your body forward...recover to a neutral stance. Paddle, paddle...step back and sink tail... reach and pull your body forward...recover to a neutral stance.

This simulates a small wave take off in that you'll be paddling along just as if you were waiting for a wave. Then, as you sink the tail, this simulates the instability, stalling, and sucking back that occurs when a wave sucks you back up the face just before releasing its energy.

It's not going to send you screaming across the water, but it's a fun way to pass the time while you're making your way to the beach after a surf session or while passing time on a leisurely paddle out.

If you're really feeling saucy, you can also shift your rear foot a few inches to one side or the other as you do this exercise to practice initiating turns both front-side and back-side.

KEEPING WATCH OVER YOUR SHOULDER

Can you paddle straight ahead while looking over your right and left shoulders or does that throw you off balance? Once you've got your paddling techniques wired, the next step is to try your paddling and board control skills while looking over your shoulder.

In flat water, practice paddling while behind you. When you get in the surf, you'll have to be able to look over your shoulder while you paddle for a wave to be aware of how fast and big the approaching wave is when it gets to you.

Try doing kick turns and flat water take-offs all while looking over your shoulder. And finally, when you're feeling really good, try it all with your eyes closed for a crash course in balance training.

Stand up paddling is so much more fun after you put in the time to learn how to control your board. Then, you can think about skillfully riding the waves without second guessing your ability to turn your board and make the drop.

Section XI.
READY FOR SURF

HAVE CONTROL, GIVE RESPECT & GET WAVES

As you refine your skills and surf with respect, soon enough, the time will come when you'll hear someone whistle or holler signaling an approaching outside set and you will be in perfect position, and you'll have the skills to turn your board around confidently and make good use of a really nice wave.

With time and practice, others will recognize your ability to control your board in a variety of conditions and before long you'll hear someone yell, "Hey, you on the stand up board…Go!" A rush of excitement will go through your veins as you realize this wave has come to you!

Before you panic and fall off your board before you even get turned around, smile and stay calm. Remember that you need to do two things to catch this wave.

First, turn the board around *and then* paddle to get the speed to drop in. If you try to do them both at the same time, you'll probably lose your composure and fall off before the wave even reaches you.

If you can keep your composure, turn the board around and paddle hard to drop in. If you're the only guy out there and the wave is sizeable, whether you make the drop or get pitched over the lip because of a super late take-off will usually be irrelevant. Either way it'll make a good show.

If the wave was big and no one was in position but you, and you went for it, and gave a good show even if it turned into a glory jump over the falls, they'll call out another one for you soon enough.

DON'T BE A COCKED PISTOL

Although it may be tempting to just keep your board pointed toward the beach so all you have to do is start paddling straight ahead when a wave comes, it's not a good idea.

First of all, you'll probably fall off trying to look over your shoulder while paddling for the incoming waves.

Secondly, this behavior usually creates discomfort for all the others in the lineup as you stand there like a cocked pistol. There's a good chance that doing this will put other surfers on edge because there's no way of knowing if or when you're going to paddle for a wave, and nobody wants to get dropped in on by someone on a big board with a carbon fiber hatchet in hand.

Thirdly, it lacks style, man.

The truth is, if you aren't able to turn your board around to catch a wave, you don't yet have the board control needed to surf with others.

PRONE-PADDLE SURFING BEFORE SUP SURFING?

Stand up paddling in flat water inevitably plants the seed of wave riding in the minds of most stand up paddlers. Even for those who have taken up the sport just for fitness, the little seed of curiosity will probably grow to the point where even those with no prior surfing experience decide to go out and chase some waves.

In my mind, this is great! The sport has opened up the relaxing thrill of surfing to many people that have never before thought of wave riding.

Even though this book covers proper surfing etiquette, padding out, getting caught inside, avoiding oncoming surfers, managing the current, watching out for other surfers, and judging wave height and power, nothing can replace first-hand experience. To fully understand the ebb, flow, and rotation of surf traffic, I think it's a great idea to spend some time on a traditional lay down paddle surfboard.

Spending time traditional prone paddle surfing will help you understand first-hand where the take-off zones are for regular surfers (so you don't steal their waves), and will give you insights into surf safety and etiquette from a regular prone-paddle surfer's point of view that cannot be taught in a book and can be learned only by experience.

Now back the question. Is it a good idea to spend time traditional prone paddle surfing before stand up paddle surfing with others?

In my opinion, it's a resounding, YES!

KISSED BY A WAVE

Okay, you've mastered the skills of paddling and turning your stand up paddle surfboard and can ride in waist high waves with confidence and skill. Now you've got that burning desire to take your stand up paddle surfing to the next level and ride a wave with some juice to it.

First, let's set the scene. This is the day. You arrive at the beach with a smile on your face and a thrill in your heart. The low grumble of sizable waves vibrates the air which travels through your ears, straight to that part of your brain that thinks about nothing but surfing.

You can taste the salt in the air and feel the mist from the whitewater on your lips. The smell of surf wax and sunscreen tickles your nose and reaffirms that you're actually there. Smiling from ear to ear you slide your arm around the glassy cool back of your board, pull it off the car, and balance it on your head.

Gripping the paddle in your other hand, you walk hypnotically to the water's edge without blinking an eye and set your board down in the sand to survey the scene. Next, you strap the leash on your ankle, peel it off and put it back on again just to hear the ripping noise that says, "It's time."

You say a little prayer and slide your board into the water for the paddle out. You go wide and easily make your way out to the break with your eyes fixated on the incoming waves. The grin on your face says it all. You are stoked simply to be in the water.

The first set of waves rolls through the lineup, head high and glassy! To keep everyone else in the water at ease, you let the next few sets go by and call out the incoming waves for the others. Then you see it, the sneaker set coming in from way outside. After making eye contact with the wave, you know this one's for you.

While everyone else is caught on the inside preparing for impact, you are in perfect position to ride this monster. You take a deep breath to stay calm and carefully maneuver the board around. Then, without looking back you start stroking strong and even.

As your board starts planing over the water's surface, all background noises fade and the only sound you hear is the gentle splashing of water coming off your paddle and lapping around nose of your board.

With a quick peek over your shoulder, you catch a glimpse of the wave looming overhead. Your feet instinctively go into a staggered stance. It's time to dig deep. Your board is lifted by the wave and you can feel yourself being sucked up to the lip. *Stroke, stroke, stroke.*

Time stands still as your board seems to lose all forward momentum from the water sucking back and up the face of the wave leaving you floating, weightless.

Gazing over the edge of a watery cliff, you give one final stroke with your paddle then, *VOOM!* Your fins engage with the surface of the wave and you're screaming down the face.

The roar and rumble of the wave breaking close behind you heightens your senses. You plant your paddle into the wave and crank a solid bottom turn that fires you straight back up to the lip of the wave or a turn off the top, followed by a re-entry sends you down into the pocket and screaming straight ahead in a blur of water and wind.

The roar of rushing water echoes through your soul like audible adrenaline. The power of the wave surges through your legs to your thumping heart until wave spits you out as you sail into the channel weightless and free with a dazed smile on your face. Your silly grin spreads from ear to ear.

You've been kissed by a wave.

READING THE WAVES

One of the beauties of surfing is that everyone has a different style and everyone has their own unique vision of the ideal wave.

On one end of the spectrum, aggressive high performance surfers are usually on the hunt for waves that are steep, fast, and strong. On the other end, more classic surfers generally prefer long mellow walls perfect for noserides and smooth, drawn out turns. The

ability to determine which wave will shape up the way you like it comes from taking the time to read the waves.

As you watch the sets of waves roll in, try to pinpoint exactly where you would want to be at the critical moment when you would drop into *your* wave. Envision yourself in that spot looking down the face of the wave and take note of how steep the drop will be at that point.

Will you drop straight down the face or will you take off at an angle? Does the lip of the wave kick up at the breaking point or does the face have a gradual slope to it? How deep will you need to be for a successful takeoff?

Take note of the speed of the incoming swells. If they are approaching quickly, you will most likely be in for quick acceleration upon takeoff. If the swells are approaching slowly, the takeoff should be smooth and easy.

Mentally envision what your stance and weight distribution will be when it's your turn to drop in. Try and calculate how early you should start paddling for the wave.

If the wave is steep and ledgy, it may take only two or three strokes, but if the approaching mountain of water is slopey and flat, you may need five or six strokes before the waves starts to carry you.

It's a lot to consider, but as you take the time to review these details, you will train your eyes to properly read the waves, recognize where the take-off spots are, and envision your ride.

POSITIONING & STABILITY

After first preparing mentally, then paddling out to the take off zone, as you prepare to catch a wave, position your board both perpendicular to the approaching waves, as close to the highest peak of the wave as possible.

On a stand up paddle surfboard it is always better to put yourself in the right position for take off the *first* time.

Shoulder hopping away from the peak could put you in the path of another surfer riding a wave. Shoulder hopping is when you catch a wave on the shoulder instead of near the breaking crest of the wave.

Taking off on a wave with the board angled straight toward the beach is the easiest take off angle when you are first starting out.

The Takeoff

Easier

More Challenging

Sometimes it may be necessary to drop in and catch a wave angled across the face of the wave right from the start. However, when you take off at an angle, the board is more likely to flip upside down exposing your fins just as you take off.

Now, if you've ever looked down at your board only to see your fins staring up at you, it's pretty darn scary. Those things are sharp and we want to keep them in the water. Your first waves shouldn't be firing rights or lefts anyway, but should be forgiving enough to allow for a straight forward take off.

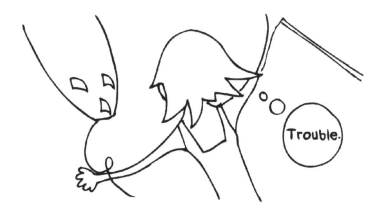

THE BACKWARD SUCK & FORWARD PUSH

In flat water, most of the instability that you used to feel came from side to side motions. When you venture out into the waves, front to back movements will be added to the side to side rocking, and therein is the challenge of maintaining control in the ocean.

As you paddle to catch your first waves on a stand up paddle surfboard, you will notice that as the face of the wave lifts you up, it may feel as if someone is moving the Earth on you. It's a feeling similar to walking around on bumpy train, during an earthquake, or standing on an airplane during turbulence.

The board may unexpectedly jerk from front to back or side to side beneath your feet, threatening to throw you off balance. Stay relaxed with your knees bent and your paddle in the water. Let the water flow under you as you focus on your basic skills. If you stiffen up, you're sure to go for a swim. Stay loose and let your board and body move with the energy of the ocean.

With a wave at your heels, you will feel the water suck you back a little as if the wave were drawing you back and in towards it. On waves of consequence, this backward pull is cannot be ignored. On smaller waves, you may or may not notice the pull. What happens is, as the wave moves forward and up, it sucks up the water directly in front of it, forcing it all over the lip.

For a stand up paddler, while you are in the shadow of the wave, it may feel like all of a sudden you are paddling in place or even backwards as if someone had grabbed the tail of your board at the most inopportune moment.

When you feel this sensation of being pulled backwards, that is when you need to bear down and paddle your hardest. If the water being sucked back into the face of the wave saps you of all your forward momentum, it's likely that the wave will pass under you and go unridden. So, keep paddling, even if it feels like you aren't going anywhere.

Next, you will feel the tail of your board begin to rise. Then, just as you reach the crest of the wave, the backward pull will quickly transfer into a forward push.

Stagger your feet a little more, use the paddle to stabilize yourself, and continue paddling until the energy of the wave sends you skimming forward.

Depending on the length and rocker of your board, you may need to shift your weight forward of the center. Then, when you feel yourself gliding, quickly shift your feet toward the back of the board to prevent the nose from getting buried the water sending you for a swim.

THE NEED FOR SPEED

There you are. You found an area where you can practice on your own without having to work around other surfers. There is a set approaching on the horizon, and judging from the leftover whitewater from the last set, you have positioned your board pointed straight toward the shore a board length or two outside of where the wave should break when it arrives.

Now you have a need for speed, enough speed to get you skimming along the surface of the water so that when the wave arrives you will easily slide down the face.

At this moment, focus on technique. Proper form will initially get you more power than frantically exerting energy. So, first, check your form.

As I mentioned earlier, focus on one thing at a time. If you think about paddling to get speed, making the drop, and riding the wave all at the same time, it's very likely that you'll lose your concentration and fall off your board before the wave even arrives.

My football coach used to say, "First, catch the ball, then run. If you think about running before you catch the ball, you're going to drop it." The principle applies here as well.

One of the frustrations that new stand up paddle surfers sometimes experience when they get in the surf is that no matter how hard they paddle, the wave passes right under them. I wasn't an exception to the rule by any means when I was first learning. The wave would come, I'd paddle like mad and it would pass right under me, sometimes throwing me off into the water.

What's the solution? Go back to the flat water, and practice paddling with more intensity. Stagger your feet, lower your center of gravity, envision the wave coming from behind, and paddle hard. Practice doing short sprints.

Through this exercise, you'll discover exactly where your feet need to be on your board for maximum paddling speed. Then, when the time comes that you need extra speed, you'll know exactly how to muster some up.

MAKING THE DROP SAFELY & TOTALLY COMMITTED

You've been counting the waves and see one that was meant for you. Now it's time to commit. Once you're clear of all other surfers and have a surety that you are not going to drop in on anyone, it's time to commit.

You kick turn to spin your board into the perfect position. You stick your paddle in the water to help stabilize yourself and maintain your current positioning until it's time to start paddling hard.

Once you are in the right spot you briefly glance over your shoulder to gauge the speed of the approaching wave and adjust your stroke accordingly.

You're now ready to make your final push to drop into the wave. Before you do so, turn your head yet again and scan both left and right to assure that you won't be dropping in on anyone and also to identify any potentially hazardous situations you may have not noticed previously.

It's time to commit. Regardless of the wave size, if you have an attitude of, "maybe this wave will take me, maybe it won't," most likely, it won't. However, if you are *committed* to getting into the wave, you're in. Bear your head down and keep your eyes on where you want to go as you deliver strong deliberate strokes.

You may have to shift your feet forward on the board a few inches to release your fins a little to start gliding down the surface of the wave. Stay focused. If the size of the wave appears bigger now than you thought it was, it's too late to chicken out, so if the coast is still clear, go for it!

Turning back now will only take you over the falls and through the spin cycle and endanger other surfers, as there's a good chance the next wave will be bigger than this one.

Focus on staying balanced and keeping proper foot positioning, and there's a good chance you'll make the drop without a problem. When you do, you'll re-live the rush of surfing over and over again and be totally stoked on your accomplishment. However, to make it all happen, you've got to be committed.

TAKE THE BLINDERS OFF

When we talk about surfing with commitment, it doesn't mean aggressively grabbing all the waves, and it doesn't mean dropping in on other surfers.

What do I mean by taking the blinders off? Have you ever seen a horse pulling a wagon or cart? The horse usually has blinders on the sides of his eyes that allow him only to see exactly what is in front of him, making the horse unaware of the surroundings.

A surfer with virtual blinders on is so focused on catching the wave in front of him or her that the stand up paddler fails to recognize if someone else had priority of the wave, for example.

If your skills are not developed to the point where you can react to the ever-changing surroundings, you should not be in the waves yet.

You should be able to paddle for a wave with total commitment but have the control and a full awareness about where all the other surfers are, and be able to quickly back off or pull out of a wave if necessary.

ATTACKING THE BOTTOM TURM

Unless you're in the mood for just straight shooting it to the beach after making the drop down the face of a wave, you'll have to change your board's direction. It's time to learn about bottom turns. An effective bottom turn is essential to making the maximum use of the power of the wave.

With today's modern surfing style, most of the attention is give to all the water throwing action above the lip of the wave. Magazines love to publish photos of guys turning hard off the top of the wave sending a spray of water into the sky. All that high flying action begins with a deep and solid bottom turn.

I'm not talking about dropping half way down the face, then cruising to the shoulder. I'm talking about riding the face from the top of the wave *all the way down* to the bottom of the wave, then powering back up the face with momentum and control.

After dropping into the wave, your board carries with it a burst of speed and momentum. A well executed bottom turn redirects all of that energy to propel you back to the top of the wave setting the stage for the remainder of the ride.

The paddle is your partner in crime when it comes to bottom turns. Due to the length, thickness, and sheer volume of stand up paddle surfboards, you will need to leverage your weight and power with the effective use of the paddle.

The first decision you'll need to make before you begin your bottom turn is whether you are going to go left or right.

Quickly scan both directions. You'll want to go in the direction where the face of the wave looks like it's going to stay open. Usually, in one direction, you'll see the lip of the wave feathering and breaking and in the other direction you'll see a smooth open road inviting you to travel down it.

Experienced surfers can usually tell if the wave is going to break left of right simply by the angle that the swell is coming in from the ocean before it even begins to peak. As you stay observant to the waves as they come though, you too will be able to train your eye to pick out the waves that are going to break near you and in your preferred direction.

WHICH WAY IS LEFT?
WHICH WAY IS RIGHT?

When I was first learning how to surf, I remember looking out on the water with a more experience surfer at my side who said to me, "Wow! Look at that right."

Having no idea what he was talking about and in a valiant effort to save face, I replied with something like, "Yeah... that's nice."

For the first time since kindergarten, I didn't know my left from my right. Now that's embarrassing!

Is a "right" a wave that goes right from the perspective of the surfer dropping in or from the perspective of the onlooker from the beach?

Here it is: A wave is considered a "right" if the wave opens up to the right from the point of view of the surfer in the water facing the beach, and a "left" is when a surfer padding for a wave drops in and goes to his or her left.

It is generally easier for regular footed surfers (those who surf with their right foot on the tail) to ride waves going right. On the flip side, it is usually easier for goofy footed surfers (those who surf with their left foot on the tail) to ride waves that go left.

Now, you've made the drop and have decided which direction you are going to go. Move your foot back toward the tail of your board. The closer your back foot is to being directly over the fins, the more nimble and responsive your board will be.

Given the great volume of a stand up paddle board, you may also have to move that back foot to the edge of the board to get enough pressure on the rail and bury it in the water, on the side touching the wave, to initiate a powerful turn. Your front foot will normally stay closer to the center line of the board in a surf stance. Keeping your front foot more centered will make for an easier recovery after making the turn.

With your back foot on the tail, bend your knees deep and keep your chin up with your eyes in the direction you want to go. Apply pressure to the tail of your board as you plant the paddle into the wave and lean on it.

FLIP THE BLADE OR LEAVE IT STRAIGHT?

There are some surfers who prefer to flip the paddle blade over and let it skim over the water with less drag. It is more common to simply leave the paddle blade in the same direction as it was when padding for the wave. This way if you need an extra push with the paddle, you can deliver one without flipping the blade over again.

WHAT TO DO WITH YOUR PADDLE WHILE SURFING

You can get a tremendous amount of leverage by transferring your weight to the blade of the paddle while riding a wave. If you ever find yourself wondering what to do with the paddle once you have dropped into a wave, just stick it in the water. You'll find something to do with it and will quickly learn to use the paddle to execute maneuvers as well as maintain balance and control in critical sections.

As your paddle skims across the water's surface, it becomes a stabilizer and a pivot point for riding and turning.

After initiating the bottom turn and effectively burying the rail of your board, if you immediately skim the paddle across the water and lean it as you drive with your legs, your weight will be transferred from the board to the paddle and the decompression of your board will propel it up and forward across the water providing a quick and smooth burst of energy complete the turn. This added energy can help power you up the face of the wave and off the top into your next turn.

Have fun with bottom turns. One of the biggest mistakes that stand up paddlers make is initiating the bottom turn too early. Ride the wave all the way to the bottom, if possible, then turn. You'll find a source of energy and power you've been overlooking.

Which side of the board should you put your paddle on throughout the turn? If you are a regular footed surfer (right foot on the tail) and are going right on a wave, try planting the paddle on the right side in the face of the wave for stability and leverage.

If you are a regular footed surfer and are going left, you'll probably leave the paddle on the right side of the board and swing the paddle behind you before leaning on it. Some switch the paddle to the left side of the board and lean on it that way as they power through the bottom turn. Try both ways and see what feels most natural for you.

LET THEM HANG: NOSERIDES

In both classic and high performance surf styles, there are few things that compare to perching yourself up on the nose of your board with nothing but the wind and the waves to greet you. Planting your feet up on the top ¼ of your board is generally considered a noseride, however, there are some who'll insist that it doesn't count unless you've got at least five toes over the nose.

Regardless of how you choose to log your tip time, after a solid bottom turn and a cross-step to the nose, you'll feel the acceleration and freedom of a genuine noseride, and you'll be hooked. Then, when you break out your round-nosed stand up paddle board, you'll constantly be looking for the right section of wave that you can lock in for a step up to the nose.

Noserides, in theory, are very simple, and with some practice will become quite natural. Here's how it all works. The first thing you'll need to know before attempting a noseride is that as you move your feet forward, your board will accelerate. Likewise, as you move your feet back, it will slow down.

In a well executed noseride, you will position the board at the crest of the wave and usually to the point where the board is just about to stall out. Then, just before your board stalls out, run up to the nose. Your forward momentum will bring your board out of the stall.

The board will speed up, lock into place and you'll be noseriding!

Stand up paddle surfboards that are straighter with less nose rocker and a big center fin lend themselves better to noseriding. Boards with wider noses are also generally more stable when you've got your toes hanging over the front. Noserides can be accomplished on more performance shaped boards with a fuller nose but require a steeper, more powerful wave.

CROSS STEPPING

So how to you get to the nose anyway? The quickest, most fluid, and stylish way to walk your board is by cross stepping to the nose and cross-stepping back to the tail.

When you're first trying your hand, er, I mean foot, at walking your board, a delicate foot shuffle may feel most comfortable and stable. However, you can run faster than you can shuffle your feet, and a foot shuffle will be too slow. It's time to learn to cross-step. Step up to the nose crossing one leg past the other, and with a quick one-two, and sometimes, three-four, until you're up on the nose. Then, when your noseride is over, cross step back to the tail to set up your next maneuver.

Cross stepping is a skill that only can be learned by practice. When I was first leaning to noseride, I was taught to just run up there and see what happens, and do it over and over again until I start to feel what works. With faith in that piece of advice, that's what I did, and it worked. There is a learning curve with plenty of falls but eventually you'll get it all dialed in and find yourself with toes over the nose and a pocket full of stoke.

Learning to noseride is like learning to ride a bike. You can get the general idea by watching others and reading about it, but when it comes down to it, you really have to be willing to just run up there over and over again until you get it right. Sometimes you'll run right off the front and other times you may stall out.

Keep at it and you'll be hanging fives and tens with the best of 'em.

FAT STAND UP PADDLE FLOATERS

I can clearly remember the first time I saw a massive stand up paddle floater. It was at the First Annual Ku Ikaika Challenge on the west side of Oahu, the first big wave stand up paddle event in history. There were many memorable waves ridden that day, and one that still sticks out in my mind was when one particular surfer rode his wave to the inside section of the wave where it really jacks up.

Just before the wave closed out on him, he made a strong bottom turn and floated up to the top of the massive foam ball that appeared to be about 12' high, rode right off the front of it, landed, and finished the wave in style.

What is a floater exactly? When the lip of the wave closes out in front of you, instead of straightening out, and letting the foam ball land behind you, you do one more bottom turn launching yourself back up the face of the wave just in time to float you and your board on top of the foam ball before dropping back into the wave.

Sometimes you can "float" over a closed out section and continue the wave on the other side. Other times, it's an extra maneuver to make the most of the wave as it closes out.

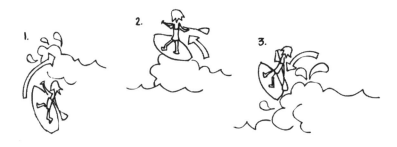

So, how is it done?

First of all, set up the maneuver with a nice powerful turn from the bottom of the wave that will take you straight up to the top. Keep you knees bent and body compact to absorb the bumps that come as you approach the disorganized whitewater at the crest of the wave. As soon as you hit the top of the wave, execute a turn right at the top, then immediately relax your legs to get your board moving across the top of the foam.

There's sort of an eerie feeling of weightlessness once you're up on top. Then, when you're ready to drop back down, shift your weight toward the front of your board and ride back down the front of the foam ball.

The trickiest part of the move is making the controlled turn at the top of the wave, essentially creating order out of disorder. Once you get this move wired, it'll probably become a favorite in your bag of tricks.

A NEW BEGINNING

When you learn any new sport or activity, it may take you a little time to get the hang of everything. In this book so far, we have gone from standing on your board to executing floaters.

If it all seems overwhelming, don't worry. In reality, for your first session or two, you may feel like you are learning to surf all over again. Essentially, you are.

With a new angle of vision, you'll have to re-learn how to judge the speed and distance of approaching waves. You'll also have to re-learn how to take off on a wave and how to turn your board.

The good news is, after a few sessions, you will begin to get proficient at the subtle skills that you'll need to surf with confidence. With each and every session, you will see a noticeable improvement in your ability. In fact, even as you sleep your mind and body will be making the connections that will turn you into an even more excellent paddler than you were when you finished your last session.

Is it worth it? Absolutely. Soon enough, you'll be riding that wave you've been dreaming about. Learn to laugh at yourself and enjoy the learning process. As you plan ahead, focus, and paddle hard, these things will all become second nature to you, and you will become an extremely skillful stand up paddle surfer.

Section XII.
TAKING ON THE ELEMENTS

SURFING IN LESS THAN PERFECT CONDITIONS

Nobody wants to be dry docked because of wind and surface texture on the water. In the early days it was thought that stand up paddling was limited only to small, clean waves with light winds at the most, and that a fully committed stand up paddler would have to give up surfing in challenging conditions. That notion is a thing of the past.

Now, there are stand up paddlers charging hard in 25-30 mph winds and massive waves, and we have yet to discover the limit. In this section, you'll learn how to surf in less than perfect conditions, namely wind and surface chop.

MANAGING THE WIND

Wind is a part of life for all surfers and can actually be a surfer's best friend. Air pressure and wind from storms thousands of miles out at sea form the waves that eventually end up at the coastline and make for an epic day on the water. When the wind on the shoreline comes from the ideal direction, it can push up the face of the wave and give perfect form to the waves at your local break.

Wind *does* force stand up paddle surfers to work harder in the lineup. When you paddle out in the wind, your body will act as a sail creating resistance, and since the only things that will prevent you from getting blown across the water are the fins on your board and the paddle in your hand, when the winds creep up to about 20 mph, you will continually be power-stroking and making small adjustments with your paddle just to remain stationary on the water.

For me, stand up paddle surfing in challenging conditions brings a certain degree of satisfaction. It also stokes me out knowing that the next time I paddle out on a glassy day, I'll be that much more skilled and confident in my ability.

The first and foremost rule for paddling in windy conditions is to be conscious of strong currents and hazards in the water. As was mentioned earlier in this book, determine what areas of the surf zone should be considered green, yellow, and red.

Without a heightened sense of awareness and advanced planning, you could easily drift off into the impact zone, into a group of surfers, out to sea, or into the rocks without even noticing until it's too late.

Exercise wisdom and caution when paddling out into the forces of nature, and if you're unsure, leave your board in the car and save it for another day. If you do paddle out, depending on how strong the winds are, your session may even turn into a stationary paddling exercise near the shore sort of like paddling on a watery treadmill. That's okay. It will increase your endurance and add power to your stroke for your next session.

BLESSED OFF-SHORE WIND

When the winds are blowing off-shore, meaning from the beach straight out to the waves, paddling out to the lineup will be a breeze. As soon as you point your board toward the horizon, the wind will blow you straight out to the ocean.

Relax and let the wind carry you out. You can use that saved energy for the powerful strokes you'll need to get into the waves as you paddle into the wind to drop in on a wave.

Your body, the paddle, and in the nose of the board will be pushing against the wind as you paddle to catch a wave. To overcome this, simply bend your knees more than normal in a staggered stance to stay low and close to your board, and position yourself slightly more forward on the board.

You will often feel as if you are paddling in a stationary position while you are paddling into the wind to catch a wave. That may very well be the case. With a sizeable wave, all the wind that hits the face of the wave will blow straight up to the lip where you are teetering on edge trying to make that drop.

Your paddling may be just enough to keep you in position until the lip of the wave comes up behind you, tipping you over the edge and sliding you down the face of the wave. Continue to paddle until you are positive that you are in the wave.

Off-shore Wind

Occasionally, a gust of wind will catch under the nose of your board and blow you backwards just as you thought you were about to make the drop. Hey, if the wind is strong enough, sometimes you'll even make the drop then get blown back up over the top of the wave throwing you off your board. If this happens, cover your head, and when you hit the water, stay under for a few extra seconds. Your board is guaranteed to be sailing through the air before crash landing somewhere between the leash attached to your ankle and about 10 feet around.

Your best bet for catching waves on a day like this would be to find small to medium waves. But hey, you never know, maybe at just the right moment the wind will die down for a second or two and allow you to drop right in for a magic ride.

Stand up paddle surfboards with more pulled-in pointed noses will also make it easier to drop in on windy days. With less surface area up front, there's less surface area to catch the wind racing up the front of the wave.

USING SIDE-SHORE WIND TO YOUR ADVANTAGE

Wind that blows sideways across the water can actually help you get into the waves with less effort and create steep and hollow wave formations. It can be really fun surfing in side shore winds and here's how it's done:

Paddle out in the channel and wait up-wind of where the waves are breaking with the nose of your board pointed into the wind. By "up-wind" I mean paddling yourself into the wind past where the wave breaks so that if you were to stop paddling, the wind would blow you back into position.

You may have to paddle in place to keep from drifting into the impact zone, so keep a steady paddle pace while you are waiting. Keep an eye on the incoming sets.

Once you've picked your wave, put a little pressure on the rail of your surfboard and let the wind turn you around and gently blow you into position for a perfect drop. You may have to drag your paddle in the water as you turn to avoid overshooting the take-off zone with a sudden gust of wind.

Then, just as the wave is upon you, power stroke with the wind at your back to gain speed. It may only take one or two digs. With your new momentum, the use of your paddle, and a little footwork, angle the board down the face of the wave exactly when the swell arrives.

You will zip down the face. Depending on the swell direction, you can carry on down the line with the wind at your back, or you can turn the board into the wind for a breezy, and sometimes hollow, section.

If you choose to surf the wave into the wind, be ready to cross step to the nose. Your weight forward will help you maintain speed and keep the nose from catching the wind underneath and flipping you off.

MAKING THE MOST OF ON-SHORE WIND

On-shore wind usually creates a soup of messy whitecaps, bumps, and texture but it's still worth a paddle out. When the wind is blowing in from the water straight towards the beach, your greatest task will be staying on your feet and paddling into the wind against the incoming wind and swell to make it out to the lineup.

The rough water will try to throw you off balance but it'll make you a stronger surfer. Find the channel where the water from the incoming waves is flowing back out to the ocean and ride that current back to the lineup.

Once you arrive at the lineup, keep going until you are well beyond where the waves are breaking, maybe 20 or 30 yards if the wind is really howling. Once you get there, as with all windy conditions, you'll have to keep paddling to maintain your position.

After you pick your wave, let the wind turn your board around so the wind is at your back and blow you down the face of the wave. Your body will act as a sail and, if the breeze is stiff enough, you may not even need to stroke to drop in. Then, once you are in the wave, ride that baby in as far as you safely can. Then, if you have the energy, paddle back out into the wind and do it all over again.

219

THE DYNAMICS OF VARIABLE WIND

If anything is going to refine your stand up paddle surfing skills, it'll be paddling out in variable, gusty winds. Your board and body will tend to spin and swirl as the wind blows from various directions mysteriously and without warning.

The current will pull the board in one direction, then the wind will blow you in the other, and you'll be dancing on, or in, the water. If you keep your paddle in the water, you can lean on it should a gust of wind hit you from one side then change direction and blindside you from the other.

Variable winds can also be a lot of fun and make for an extremely dynamic session. As the swells come in off the water from one direction, from time to time the wind will blow from exactly the right direction, pushing up the face and opening up the wave for an epic ride.

Although these conditions are less predictable, if you're patient enough, chances are eventually the stars are going to align and you'll score a perfect *go home* wave. You know -- the wave you catch that was so good that you could just call it a day right there and go home smiling. Yep, that's the "go home" wave.

BE THANKFUL FOR THE WIND

Surfing in the wind can be a rockin' good time. It provides plenty of opportunities for endurance training, muscle strengthening and confidence building. As always, surf with a smile on your face and charge hard. In actuality, on a calm day you may find yourself wishing there was a little breeze to spice things up a bit.

Wind usually gets a bad rap, but without wind there would be no waves. So when the wind is howling, thank the wind for bringing the waves, then paddle out and catch some.

Section XIII.
WIPEOUT SURVIVAL GUIDE

WIPEOUTS & GETTING CAUGHT INSIDE

If you plan on catching waves, it is inevitable that you'll have some wipeouts and eventually find yourself stuck right in the impact zone. This is called "getting caught inside."

When you learn how to handle wipeouts and what to do when you get caught inside, you will be comfortable playing in waves that make others uneasy and unlikely to paddle out because of the fear of getting caught inside.

We've all seen it. It's the swell of the year and there is a line of wave watchers on the beach. Half of them have boards on their cars and are debating whether or not to paddle out while the others are just enjoying the show. There are a dozen guys or less out in the water patiently waiting for the set waves.

The wave watchers can see the swells looming on the horizon. The surfers in the water can sense the waves' presence and that's all they need to start a full sprinted paddle into position.

As the mountain of water approaches and surfers start getting sucked up the giant face of the wave, it seems only logical to paddle over the beast before it swallows everyone. In that instance, a local favorite turns his board, and after two strokes and a short airdrop, that brother is riding the wave.

The silence is broken by a chorus of, "Ooooh!" Moments later, the wave closes out on the inside and instead of kicking out over the back, the surfer pulls the fattest floater of the season. Up...and...*BLAM*...down! He sticks it. The clicking and whizzing of cameras on the beach is muffled by rumbling waters as our surf hero raises his hands triumphantly just before being quickly swallowed by a wall of whitewater from the next wave that could easily hide a cement truck.

Does our hero retire for the day after the hard whitewater beating? No way! He pops his head out of the water completely stoked and paddles out for another round. The energy of the wave feeds his soul and the spin cycle at the end was the grand finale to a memorable ride.

TROUBLE AHEAD?
SAFETY FIRST

As always, the first thing to have in mind when you are about to wipe out is safety for those around you and yourself. As was mentioned earlier, a big board on a long leash can travel farther than you think.

When it seems like you're going to wipe out, quickly scan down the line where you're headed and steer clear of any surfers or swimmers in the water even if it means straightening out and getting pounded by the whitewater. You may go through the washer but there will always be another wave and nothing is worth putting you or those around you in danger.

SURVIVING WIPEOUTS WITH A PADDLE

What should you do with your paddle in a wipeout? The answer is simple: hold onto it. But if you can't hold onto it for some reason, the paddle will float to the surface where usually you should be able to find it.

It's a good idea to put a strip or two of brightly colored tape on your paddle to make it more visible in the whitewater. Some put one strip near the handle and another on the shaft near the blade.

The truth is, when you have a good grip on your paddle, unless it's a cracking bomb of a wave, rarely will a wave pull it out of your hand.

In actuality, the only time you'll probably let go of it is if you feel like you need to use two hands to swim to the surface after getting pushed down really deep. What you should be more concerned with is keeping the paddle under control so that when the foam ball comes down on you, you don't knock yourself silly with your own equipment.

The paddle is a great tool to have when Mother Nature decides it's time for you to ride a wave underwater. First off all, since it floats, you'll always know which way is up.

After a heavy wipeout, where prone paddle surfers might climb their leash to get directed toward the surface, stand up paddlers can get headed in the right direction simply by following the upward pull of the paddle.

227

Secondly, when it occurs to you that you're about to wipe out or get swallowed by another wave after being caught inside, make sure your nose and mouth are clear of water so you'll be able to get a full breath.

If you ask me, there's nothing wrong with holding your nose from time to time. I sometimes hold my nose when I'm already caught in the impact zone and I have to brace myself for impact from the rest of the set waves that I'm about to take on the head. However, when the water's really churning, your arms will be all over the place with water up your nose and cycling through your sinuses underwater anyway.

After filling your lungs with air, hold the paddle with two hands, one where the blade and the shaft meet, and the other about arm's length in front of it. With two hands on the shaft, it is less likely that the paddle will spin out of control under water.

Next, tuck the paddle blade under your armpit and behind you with the blade horizontal and the handle facing forward. In this position, as the wave pulls you along underwater, lift up on the handle and put your weight back on the blade of the paddle. This will plane you right up to the surface.

Even in bigger waves you'll be spending less time below the surface when you learn to use your paddle to control your direction underwater. Furthermore, with the blade in control and behind you, you aren't going to knock yourself or ding your board with it. I'm not saying that this is a sure fire technique to handle every wipeout, but so far it's worked well for me.

On that note, remember that the paddle blade can be as sharp as the fins on your board so do your best keep it under control. Try to hold the paddle with 2 hands if possible. If you have only one hand on the paddle, you run the risk of twisting your arm if the water decides to take your paddle for a spin. In short, when you see that you're about to go down, simply tuck the paddle blade under your arm and behind you, then enjoy the ride.

YOU'RE CAUGHT INSIDE: NOW WHAT?

After a wipeout, and it's not uncommon to get stuck in the impact zone where the current and waves prevent you from paddling back to the lineup. The waves may seem to be coming from several directions and the walls of whitewater may seem to never end.

It happens all the time and if you know what to do before you find yourself there, you'll be able to stay calm, collected, and will be able to find your way back to the beach or back out to the lineup.

Remember when we talked about not peeing into the wind? First of all, locate your board and position it in such a way that it will not hit you when the next wave arrives. Make sure it's between you and the beach, not you and the wave, or you may be kissing your board when the next wave bears down on you.

Then, unless there is immediate danger that needs to be avoided, and unless there is someone within striking distance of your board, simply relax and wait out the set.

If you have the time, clear your nose and sinuses of any foamy water. Stay calm and take a deep breath. Then, flip your board upside down. With your board upside down, the oncoming wave usually rolls over the board. Personally, I've found that if my board is right side up when the foam ball hits, it usually drags me along underwater for what sometimes feels like an eternity. However, if I manage to get the board flipped upside down first, the pull is shorter.

230

Also, if you can push your board away from you so that the leash is totally extended when the whitewater rolls over, the strain on whichever ankle wearing the leash will be lessened, as will the wear and tear on your equipment. With the leash fully extended, the wave will simply pull on the leash. On the contrary, if your leash is not fully extended on impact, there will be a sharp tug on your ankle, which will also increase the chances of leash breakage.

Take a deep breath and turn around with your back to the oncoming wave. Next, get your paddle in a safe position, straighten your body like a pencil and try and sink down below the surface as deep as possible before the wave rolls over you. The deeper you can get before the wave passes over, the less turbulent the water will be for you on impact.

Unless there are rocks nearby, the waves will wash you in where the waves aren't as strong. If there are surfers between you and the beach and there is even the slightest chance that your board might hit someone else, use either the Tail Grab or Leash Wrap to keep your board tethered. We'll go over those in the coming pages.

Again, the most important thing is to stay relaxed. If you panic, you will use more oxygen and will not be thinking clearly about what you need to do to get back to safety.

RETAINING YOUR BOARD: TAIL GRAB

This technique for retaining your board can be done in small to medium size surf. Here's how it's done. First, spin the board around to where the board is "down wave" from you and you can get your hand on the tail. Next, place the palm of your hand flat on the deck of your board about 4 to 6 inches from the tail of your board.

Just before the whitewater rolls over you and your board, push the tail down and pull the board back toward you as sharply as you can all in one motion. The downward push should sink the tail enough to initiate sort of a tail-first duck dive, keeping the board from getting yanked away.

The sharp backward pull will somewhat counter the initial tug that happens right when the wave hits you from behind. Although it isn't necessary, a tail block or traction pad on your board will greatly help with this technique as it will increase your ability to grip the board.

If the wave is big, you probably won't be able to retain your board using the Tail Grab. In this case, the Leash Wrap should do the trick.

ANOTHER TECHNIQUE: LEASH WRAP

This technique is just plain awesome. It will give you a solid two handed grip on both the paddle and board, preventing it from hitting others that may also be caught inside.

Again, if there is absolutely no danger of your board getting swept into someone who is "down wave" from you, relax and just let your board "blow in the wind". Then, when there's a break in the waves, recover your board and be on your way.

However, if you need to hold on to your board to prevent possibly injuring someone else, try the Leash Wrap. It's really quite simple. Hold your paddle in one hand near the middle of the paddle shaft. With your other hand, wrap the leash around and around the shaft six to eight times as tightly as possible.

Then, when the whitewater hits, grip the paddle with one hand on either side of the leash wrappings. When the foam ball rolls over you, the wave will pull the board and cinch up the leash that is wrapped around your paddle shaft. You'll go for an underwater ride while you're holding on with two hands. It's sort of like refusing to let go of the handle while being dragged along on your stomach behind a waterskiing boat.

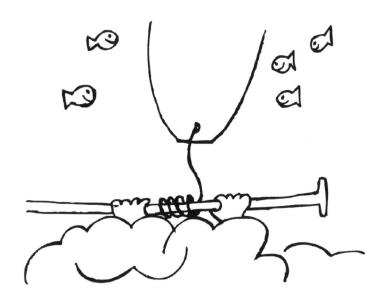

Take care to avoid getting your fingers caught in the leash wrappings as they cinch up around your paddle. They may tighten irregularly and could slide from side to side pinching your fingers. While there is a chance of pinching your fingers, for me, I'd rather get my fingers pinched any day than whack a fellow surfer.

AFTER THE SET WAVES HAVE PASSED

After the set waves have passed, and you're still in the impact zone, determine what will be the easiest way back to the channel, the beach or the lineup. When I say "the easiest" I really mean *the easiest;* not what seems like the shortest distance and not the way that you used to paddle out on your shortboard. Take the path of least resistance.

Taking the easiest way around may mean getting washed all the way back to the shore, and you may even decide to go all the way to the sand, get out of the water and carry your board back to where you need to be.

As soon as there is a break in the action, climb up to your knees and stroke toward the channel before the next wave hits. It may take some time, and you may only get in one or two strokes before the next wave hits but I've found that if I stay calm, be patient, and take action, I'll make it to safety without too much trouble. Stay calm, be alert, be patient but not lazy, and keep moving.

Some stand up paddle surfers prefer to lie down and arm paddle out of the impact zone. They tuck the paddle blade under their chest with the handle pointing up and forward. I have also seen the others stick the paddle between their legs and knee paddle with their arms from point A to point B.

You can give these techniques a try if you'd like. I personally feel out of control without at least one hand on the paddle, but I'm not everyone. Even in small surf, if the paddle comes loose and knocks you or someone else in the face or head, it could sure leave a mark.

LOSING YOUR BOARD IN THE SURF

Imagine riding a perfect wave until it closes out and takes you under, then for some strange reason you don't feel the usual tug and pull from your board. Upon surfacing, it's likely that you'll see your board bouncing in the surf on its way back to the beach without you. Your leash broke.

On the lighter side, almost every seasoned surfer has plenty of stories about breaking a leash and the long swim in, and now you too will have one to tell. First of all, stay calm. The current and waves will probably take you the same general direction that they took your board.

If you see your board, swim to it. If not, swim toward the shore and you'll probably find it washed up somewhere. In general surfers always help each other out catching each others boards and pulling them up on the sand to keep them from bouncing on the rocks.

Keep in mind that without your board, you are almost invisible to other surfers. Stay aware of other wave riders and assume that they don't see you. When a surfer is coming down the line on a wave, always swim behind the approaching surfer, never in front.

236

If a surfer is headed toward you and it's clear that they don't see, duck under the water and swim for the bottom of the ocean as fast as you can to avoid contact with the oncoming board and sharp fins. Those things are as sharp as razors when they're traveling through the water.

SWIMMING WITH YOUR PADDLE

Every stand up paddler should be practiced at swimming with their paddle. The time may come that you find yourself out on the water with a paddle but without a board. There are several ways to swim with your paddle. In this section we'll cover three of them. I encourage you to experiment and adapt them to your local surf conditions and what you feel comfortable doing.

One way to swim with your paddle is to hold the paddle with two hands, the same way you would hold it if you were knee paddling, one hand close to the blade and the other about half way up the shaft.

With a firm grip on the paddle, stroke yourself in the direction you need to go as if you were paddling a swamped canoe. It's slow going this way but it doesn't use too much energy, especially because your paddle floats.

For me, I use this technique for short distances where timing isn't critical and I can lazily make my way to my board or back to shore.

A second way to swim with a paddle is to hold the paddle in one hand and side stroke to safety. Hold the paddle in your leading hand. This will allow you to cup your other hand and push the water in short gliding bursts with a scissor kick.

A third way to get to safety is to float on your back, hold your paddle close to your chest with the blade resting near your stomach and the shaft extending up past either shoulder, and kick in the direction that you need to go.

Depending on the amount of turbulence in the water, you may be able to hold the paddle with one hand and use the other to help move you along more quickly. The great thing about this method is that you'll be facing the incoming waves as you paddle toward the shore so you can keep an eye on other surfers and incoming sets. The downside is that you don't see where you're going and might get off track or you could lose sight of your loose board.

Along with these three techniques, there are some who wrap the paddle around their leg in a way similar to how you would climb a rope in gym class or slide down a fireman's pole.

I have also heard of some sticking the paddle shaft or blade down their shorts while they swim. It'll be a snow day in Hawaii before you catch me doing that, but I guess it works for some.

I can just see myself now rolling out of control though the whitewater taking a wicked shot to the groin every time I go head over heels. *Whack! Whack! Whack! Whack!* Trouble.

If all of this stuff is too awkward, you can always just push your paddle out in front of you while you swim after it.

To conclude this section, wipeouts and whitewater are all part of the program with stand up paddle surfing. If you're serious about learning to ride waves, you going to fall and you may take a few tumbles through the spin cycle, but that's okay.

Sometimes you'll make it back to the lineup and think, "Wow! I just got hammered on the inside!" Shake it off and do it again and again and again. You are part of a stoked group of surfers that can fall down smiling, get up smiling, and never be discouraged. Awesome!

Section XIV.
THE CONCLUSION

You made it! It has been a blast taking you through the sport of stand up paddle surfing. We've talked about everything from etiquette and safety to board construction to paddling technique and wipeout survival.

Now it's your turn to get out and use what you've learned. So, what's next? Get out there and have some fun.

Keep this book on your coffee table, toilet tank, bed stand, or wherever you contemplate life and mind-surf the waves of your dreams. Refer to it often. Sometimes it just takes one little tip that makes a huge difference.

If you've done nothing more than reading this book, I'm confident that you have already become a better surfer. Professional athletes know that first you visualize it, then you make it a reality. I hope you've enjoyed this mind-surfing adventure with me.

It doesn't matter if you are old or young, big or small, a newbie or an experienced waterman or waterwoman, with the right equipment and good instruction, anyone can jump on a stand up board and paddle away stoked for life.

Your experience with stand up paddle surfing is going to be a never-ending journey loaded with challenge and excitement. Anyone can do it and the thrill never ends.

For many, stand up paddle surfing revives the magic of the first time we learned how to surf. It brings back the days when nobody cared how big the wave was or even if you caught a wave at all. It transports us back to the days when it was all about the smiles.

On a final note, some of the greatest surfers in the world have grown this sport and brought it where it is today. These legendary surfers have set a precedent of respect and reverence to the sport of stand up paddle surfing.

Please share that responsibility as a paddle surfer to continue those traditions of respect to preserve the good name of the sport and share the stoke of stand up paddle surfing.

Peace and Aloha.

Section XV.
THE FITNESS APPENDIX

REALLY GOING FOR IT WITH MODERATION

While you're learning to paddle, and as you're developing those muscles specifically associated with the sport, really go for it . . . with moderation. Let me explain.

When you're first getting started it's a good idea to limit your water time to about 30 minute sessions. Also, remember to stretch all your muscles before and afterward.

You have no idea how many injury stories start with, "I was just going for a quick one and didn't stretch." I too have one of those stories under my belt. Maybe it's a right of passage! Or, maybe not.

You'll be using new muscles and you don't want to damage those that you have rarely used until now. However, when you *are* in the water, make the most of it. Paddle like you mean it. Don't fear the falls, and be sure to keep a smile on your face.

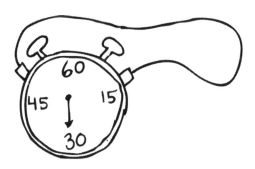

246

CROSS TRAINING AT HOME

If you want to add more power to your surfing, general resistance and strength training, and other cross training workouts will help you get there. Stand up paddle surfing uses so many different muscle groups that it's hard to go wrong when putting together an exercise program.

Most of your power and stability will initially come from your legs, so they are a good place to start, followed by your stomach, back, arms, shoulders, and neck.

If you want a quick, generalized workout for the whole body, the circuit training that you'll find at most gyms and fitness centers is an excellent compliment to stand up paddle surfing.

Circuit training is usually composed of about 10 to 15 weight training machines that are meant to be used successively. You go from one exercise to the next. The whole circuit usually takes 20 to 30 minutes and targets all the major muscle groups.

Now, if you're like me and don't have the time or patience to go to the gym and work out, or if you don't have quick access to a large body of water for regular paddling, there are plenty of exercises you can do at home to train for stand up paddling. Let's take a look at some of them. . .

LOWER BODY STRENGTH TRAINING

Of course, before you begin any workout routine, check with your doctor first. It's also a good idea to take a stand up paddle lesson to make sure you're paddling with proper form.

If lessons aren't an option where you live, have someone take some photos or shoot some video of you paddling. Then, get on the internet or order a stand up paddle video and compare your posture and technique with those on the video, and adjust your form if necessary.

If you start developing muscle memory with poor form or posture, it's going to be tough breaking those bad habits down the road. Now, let's learn some exercises.

Bicycle Crunches: Lie on your back with your lower back pressed to the floor. Place your hands lightly behind your head and bring your knees up to a 45 degree angle. Lift your shoulder blades off the ground and touch your right knee to your left elbow, then your left knee to your right elbow. Do 3 sets of 30 repetitions.

Calf Raises: (Calves) With the balls of both feet on the edge of a stair or small ledge raise and lower your heels in controlled and fluid up and down motions while using one hand on a chair to help you keep

248

your balance. As this becomes easy for you, repeat the same exercise on one foot only. Then repeat the exercise without using your hands for balance. Your balance will improve and your calf muscles will thank you.

Calf Squats: (Calves) This is an exercise that I found targets many of those little, hard-to-condition muscles that make a world of difference for a stand up paddler. First, bend your knees slightly so that you are in a half-squatting position. Then, raise your heels off the floor.

This is basically a calf raise in a half-squatting position. As you progress, lower your center of balance by squatting down even further while you repeat the calf raise.

Front Lunges: (Buttocks and Quadriceps) This exercise is a literal pain in the butt because it works your behind. Take a big step forward with one foot and drop your other knee straight down until it is 2-3 inches above the ground. Your back knee, hip, and shoulder should all be aligned.

Push off the front foot and repeat on the other side. It is very important to keep your torso upright throughout the movement to minimize stress on your back. Do 3 sets of 15-20 repetitions then grab yourself an ice-cream cone when you finish. You'll deserve it.

Squats: (Quadriceps) Stand with your feet about shoulder width apart with your hips back. Lower your hips down and back while keeping your back flat and chest facing forward, similar to sitting back into a chair. Focus on smooth, fluid, and balanced motions.

Don't lean forward or thrust your chest out over your knees and don't let your knees go over your toes to prevent stress on your joints. Stay off the balls of your feet. The force comes from the middle of the foot to the heel.

Do 3 sets of 15 repetitions. Good form will strengthen your quads and increase your balance and power. Maybe you can even get one of your friends to pull a rug out from under you while you're doing this to simulate the waves. . .

. . . or maybe not.

Sit-ups: *(Abdominals)* As you do your sit-ups, touch your right shoulder to your left knee, and then touch your left shoulder to your right knee. This will really take care of business in your mid-section and will keep you in top abdominal shape for your next paddle out.

Back Extensions: *(Lower Back)* Have a friend hold your legs as you lie on a bed or bench face down with your upper half of your body (hips and up) hanging off the edge. With your hands crossed behind your head, extend your torso up and back, then relax and repeat in sets of 5-10.

Superman: *(Lower Back)* Lay flat on your stomach with your arms extended straight out in front of you and your legs straight out behind. Lift legs and arms simultaneously off the ground 6-7 inches in a slow and controlled movement and hold for 30 seconds. Repeat 10-12 times.

Knee Hangs: *(Obliques)* This will strengthen your obliques (the side of your abs) that will help with power strokes. With your paddle held above your head and your feet shoulder-width apart, lift one knee and hip by flexing your obliques. Hold for a couple of seconds before switching sides.

UPPER BODY RESISTANCE TRAINING

Push Ups: It may sound simplistic, but push ups are an excellent exercise for stand up paddle conditioning. Rather than targeting a specific muscle, push ups condition entire muscle groups that work together when you're paddling.

Assume the push up position with your wrists directly under your shoulders with your shoulders, hips, and knees all in alignment. Keep your abs tight, back flat, and try not to sag at your hips. Lower your chest to an inch or two off the ground, then extend your arms bringing you back to the starting position. Do 3 sets of 15-20 repetitions.

Tricep Dips: *(Triceps)* Arrange two benches or chairs across from each other. Place the palms of your hands shoulder-width apart on a bench or chair behind you and your heels on an opposing bench or chair in front of you with your backside completely off the ground. Lower your body until your triceps (the back of your upper arms) are parallel to the floor. Straighten your arms and repeat. Each repetition should take about 5 seconds. Push up the first second and lower slowly for the next four.

Dumbbell Lifts: *(Biceps)* While seated and with a dumbbell or something heavy like a can of corn or a brick in hand, rest your elbow on your inner thigh and bring that dumbbell up to your chest in controlled motions. If you find yourself yanking, pulling, and moving your back, your dumbbell is probably too heavy.

Front raises: *(Front Deltoids - Shoulders)* With a dumbbell in each hand, stand with your feet shoulder width apart with your back straight. Keeping your arms straight, alternate raising each dumbbell up until it is level with your shoulders. Do not rock your upper body to throw the dumbbell into position.

One arm rows: *(Major muscle groups of the back and rear deltoids of shoulders)* Place your right knee at a 90 degree angle on a bench and your right hand resting on top of a bench leaving your left foot on the floor. With a dumbbell in your left hand, pull the weight straight up toward your chest using your back muscles. Be sure to keep your back flat and still throughout the exercise and avoid rotating your hips and shoulders. Repeat on the other side.

These exercises will help keep your muscles toned and in shape for stand up paddling. If you're able to jump in the water regularly, paddling is the best training you can do. Just paddle everywhere. If you're out paddling in the wind and choppy water, then when things calm down, your session will be as easy as a walk in the park.

As a side note, if you do choose to paddle out in challenging conditions, please do so with caution and go with a friend. Strong offshore or side shore winds can carry even the strongest paddlers out to sea or way down the coast.

Section XVI.
GLOSSARY OF KEY TERMS

- **2+1 Fin Setup:** The fin arrangement where the center fin is longer than the two side fins.
- **Barrel:** When the wave pitches over making a big sweet tube. You can see a *barrel* from the beach and you can get *barreled* while you're surfing.
- **Beach Break:** A location where the waves break on the beach. Usually sandy bottom
- **Blade:** The big flat end of that stick you're paddling with.
- **Bomb:** A big mamma wave that usually sounds like a bomb going off when the lip comes over and hits the water. *Boom!*
- **Carbon Fiber:** Synthetic material with a high strength-to-weight ratio often used in paddles and some surfboards.
- **Channel:** The path of least resistance the water follows as it returns to the ocean after the waves bring it in. Waves don't usually break in the channel.
- **Cheater Five:** Five toes over the nose, but you're really stretching it to get them there.

- **Cuff:** The part of the leash that attaches to your ankle or calf.
- **Current:** Water moving like a river in the ocean.
- **Deck:** The top surface of the board.
- **Dihedral Blade:** Paddle blade with a spine on the power side of the blade to channel the water to the sides of the blade.
- **Ding:** 1) A hole in your board. 2) The act of putting hole in a board. *I just dinged my board on that rock. Now I have to get that ding fixed.*
- **Down the Line:** Describes your movement across the face of the wave toward the shoulder of the wave to the channel.
- **Drop In:** 1) The instant you slide down the face of the wave. *I was about to drop in on the wave when . . .* 2) When you cut off another surfer who was already on the wave. *Did you see that guy drop in on that girl? That was dangerous.*
- **Duck Dive:** Traditional shortboard surfing technique where the surfer hold the sides of the board with 2 hands and push the nose of the board under an oncoming wave to duck under and come out the back side of the wave.

- **Epoxy:** A type of resin used to adhere the fiberglass to the board. Epoxy is the most common resin used on stand up paddle boards. *Note: Never use polyester resin on an epoxy board. It will eat right through the foam.*

- **Face:** The steep water wall on the front side of the wave.

- **Floater:** Surfing maneuver where you ride the board up on the ball of whitewater before dropping back into the face of the wave.

- **Fins:** Those sharp things on the bottom of your board that stick down in the water.

- **Glass:** The action of wrapping a surfboard core with fiberglass and resin. *It took 3 weeks for them to glass my board. They did a nice glass job on my board.*

- **Glasser:** The guy who puts the fiberglass and resin on your board.

- **Grabber:** A surfer who grabs all the waves. Surfing out of turn and not respecting the flow of the lineup. *Don't be a grabber.*

- **Handle:** The small end of that stick you're paddling with.

- **Hang Five:** Five toes hanging over the nose.

- **Hang Ten:** Ten toes hanging over the nose.
- **Hard Rails:** When the board's edges are turned down sharply they are considered hard. *That board has hard rails (or a sharp edge).*
- **Indexed Shaft:** An oval-shaped paddle shaft.
- **Kick Turn:** Sinking the tail before turning the board with a big swooping stroke.
- **Late Drop:** When you take off on the wave in a really steep critical section rather than easing into the wave early. *Nate didn't make the late drop and got launched over the falls.*
- **Leash:** Sometimes called a leg rope. A big long stretchy cord that attaches your board to your leg. Some leashes are meant to attach at your ankle and some at your calf.
- **Lineup:** 1) The spot where you line up to catch a wave. 2) The collective group of people waiting in a certain spot to catch waves.
- **Lip:** The leading part of the wave that pitches forward as it breaks.
- **Longboarder:** A lay down surfer that rides a board several feet longer than the rider.
- **Nose:** The very front of the board.

- **Noseride:** Perching yourself on the front ¼ of your board. Some say it doesn't count unless your toes are over the nose.
- **Off-Shore Wind:** When it's blowing from the beach out to the ocean.
- **On-Shore Wind:** When it's blowing from the ocean to the beach.
- **Over the Falls:** When you miss the take off and the wave sucks you over the front of the wave like tumbling you over a big waterfall.
- **Parallel Stance:** Standing on your board with both feet pointed forward about shoulder width apart.
- **Pitch:** 1) When the lip throws over to make the wave break. *The wave pitched right when I took off.* 2) When you get thrown over the front of the wave from the top. *I got pitched and fell a long way before hitting the bottom of the wave.*
- **Point Break:** A location where waves refract off a jetty or point creating a peeling wave.
- **Plug:** Also called leash plug. This is where the string is tied to which then attaches to the leash.

- **Pocket:** The "sweet spot" of the wave that is as close as you can get to the breaking part of the wave.
- **Polyester:** A slick fabric great for disco dancing pants. Also, the type of resin normally used to stick fiberglass to traditional lay down paddle surfboards.
- **Quad:** Describes a four-fin arrangement or a board built to be ridden with four fins. *That board is a quad. It has a quad fin setup.*
- **Quiver:** Your personal set of boards to choose from before you head out on the water.
- **Rail:** The side edges of the board.
- **Rail Saver:** The end of the leash that attaches to the board. It's called a rail saver because it prevents the leash itself from banging on the rails of your board.
- **Rocker:** The upward curve of either the nose or the tail of your board.
- **Section:** Different areas of the wave are called sections. *After making the drop the wave flattened out but I still made it to the next section.*
- **Shaft:** The long pole between the handle and the blade of your paddle.

- **Shaper:** The person who turns that big block of foam into a sleek piece of watercraft we call a stand up paddle surfboard.

- **Shoulder:** The part of the wave that is furthest from the breaking part of the wave. The shoulder usually flattens out at the channel.

- **Side-Shore Wind:** When it's blowing sideways across the beach and the water.

- **Single Fin:** The fin setup where there is just one fin in the center box.

- **Shortboarder:** A lay down surfer that rides a short pointy board.

- **Soft Rails:** When the board's edges are round without any edge they are considered soft.

- **Snap:** Bringing the board as vertical as possible at the lip of the wave and whipping it back down the face.

- **Staggered Stance:** Standing on your board with one foot in front of the other.

- **Staples:** What Nate got 14 of in the scalp after getting hit by the fin of an oncoming board.

- **Stoke:** That indescribable feeling that rushes through your whole being at the mere thought of stand up paddling.

- **String:** The little string between the leash plug on your board and the rail saver part of your leash.

- **Surf Stance:** Standing on your board with one foot back on the tail and the other in the mid section of the board. Used for surfing and kick turning the board.

- **T-Grip:** Paddle handle shaped like a T.

- **Tail:** The very back end of the board.

- **Take Off:** The instant you catch a wave. Synonymous with "drop in". *Did you see her take off on that wave?*

- **Thruster Setup:** The fin arrangement where all three fins are almost equal in size and the center fin is pushed all the way to the back of the fin box.

- **Variable Wind:** When the wind keeps changing directions on you.

- **Caught Inside:** When you are stuck in the wave impact zone.

- **Whitewater:** That ball of white foamy mess that comes rolling through after the wave has broken.

- **Wipeout:** Any time the wave swallows you alive.

ABOUT THE AUTHOR

Nate Burgoyne is the founder and editor of the digital magazine, *Stand Up Paddle Surfing Magazine (www.supsurfmag.com)*, the world's first stand up paddle publication.

Nate continues to write numerous articles about the sport, review equipment, host an online stand up paddle radio show, and has the privilege of interviewing some of the greatest watermen and women.

He got his first stand up paddle board in 2006 before the mass production of stand up paddle boards and was instantly hooked.

Nate is also co-founder of *Rainbow Watersports Adventures (www.rainbowwatersports.com)* stand up paddle school on the North Shore of Oahu and has personally taught hundreds of people of all ages and abilities how to successfully stand up paddle.

Nate was born in Hawaii on Oahu's North Shore where he currently resides with his wife and kids, and enjoys surfing, paddling, diving and fishing.

He will forever be in awe at the beauty of the land, the aloha of the people, and the blessing it is to be part of such an amazing place.

To contact Nate Burgoyne directly, please email nate@standuppaddlebook.com. Nate Burgoyne is available for interviews, signings, and barbeques.

SPECIAL THANKS!

Thanks to my parents who have always supported me in all the crazy adventures that I have pursued. And thanks to my wife who is my best friend and "partner in crime" in all of our exciting pursuits.

Mahalo to Blane Chambers and Austin Yonehiro of Paddle Surf Hawaii for their encouragement, friendship, and to Blane for hooking me up with my first board out of his garage years ago. A special thanks to paddle builders Dave and Meg Chun of Kialoa (www.kialoa.com) for their friendship and support. Also, thanks to Nikki Gregg of NRG Lifestyle Fitness (www.nikkigregg.com) for her friendship and for editing the fitness sections.

A huge thanks to the local surfers for the aloha they extended to me as I went through the stand up paddle learning curve in pursuit of the sport I have come to love.

And finally, a huge thanks to all the pioneers of stand up paddling both in the spotlight and behind the scenes that have dedicated themselves to the growth and progression of the sport and have made it possible for someone like me to make stand up paddling a part of my life. Thank you.

NOTES:

Super Awesome Bonus.

Join *The Stand Up Paddle Book Crew* for FREE and choose a FREE stand up paddle sticker while supplies last! To get yours, get online and go to:
www.standuppaddlebook.com/crew
More details on the next page.

Contact Us

For general inquiries and bulk orders please email info@lavarockpublishing.com or write to:
P.O. Box 706 Haleiwa, HI 96712.

To contact the author, email:
nate@standuppaddlebook.com.

The Next Edition

What would you like to see in the next edition? Your comments, suggestions, and ideas are greatly appreciated! Email your ideas and requests to nate@standuppaddlebook.com.

You are invited to join
The Stand Up Paddle Book Crew!

Your membership is FREE and you can choose your FREE sticker!

Simply turn on your computer and go to:
www.standuppaddlebook.com/crew

Now you can read *The Stand Up Paddle Book* with other stand up paddlers around the world online. I'm serious! No joke! Really!!!

This is a book without covers!

Every chapter of this book has its own discussion where you can comment, ask questions, and share your own personal insights and thoughts with other readers as you read this book. Pretty sweet!

Bonus! As the lucky purchaser of this book, when you join *The Stand Up Paddle Book Club* you will also choose your FREE STAND UP PADDLE STICKER while supplies last!

It's easy to get your choice of sticker and Free Membership. Simply go to:

www.standuppaddlebook.com/crew

The Stand Up Paddle Book

The Stand Up Paddle Book

LRP

Lava Rock Publishing

Haleiwa - Oahu - Hawaii